U0473522

海外藏中国艺术品
OVERSEAS CHINESE ART SELECTION

绘画卷·宋(下)
PAINTINGS · SONG (2)

本书编写组 编著
Compiled by Editorial Team

郭怀宇 本卷主编
Edited by Guo Huaiyu

NEWSTAR PRESS
新星出版社

图书在版编目（CIP）数据

海外藏中国艺术品.绘画卷.宋.下：汉英对照/郭怀宇主编；本书编写组编著.-- 北京：新星出版社，2024.12

ISBN 978-7-5133-5440-0

Ⅰ.①海… Ⅱ.①郭… ②本… Ⅲ.①中国画-中国-宋代-图录 Ⅳ.① K870.2

中国国家版本馆 CIP 数据核字 (2024) 第 056595 号

海外藏中国艺术品 绘画卷·宋（下）

本书编写组 编 著
郭 怀 宇 本卷主编

责任编辑 李文彧　　　**特约编辑** 丁文文
英文审校 韩 华　　　　**责任校对** 刘 义
装帧设计 冷暖儿　　　　**责任印制** 李珊珊

出 版 人 马汝军
出版发行 新星出版社
　　　　　（北京市西城区车公庄大街丙3号楼8001　100044）
网　　址 www.newstarpress.com
法律顾问 北京市岳成律师事务所
印　　刷 河北尚唐印刷包装有限公司
开　　本 889mm×1194mm　1/16
印　　张 12
字　　数 300千字
版　　次 2024年12月第1版　2024年12月第1次印刷
书　　号 ISBN 978-7-5133-5440-0
定　　价 268.00元

版权所有，侵权必究。如有印装错误，请与出版社联系。
总机：010-88310888　　传真：010-65270449　　销售中心：010-88310811

出版说明

按中国文物学会统计，鸦片战争以来流失海外的中国文物超过一千万件。这些文物是中国文物重要而特殊的组成部分，除其历史、文化、艺术等方面价值，更因其所凝结的民族情感而备受各界关注。

近年来，中国政府积极推动文物追索，国内外学界也涌现出一批新的研究成果，文物流失研究方兴未艾。但受诸多因素限制，海外文物归国面临着许多实际困难，能追回的仍只是很少一部分。在此情况下，加强中外合作、开展联合研究，通过出版、数字化等方式让更多人有机会了解相关资料和研究成果，成了推动流失文物"活起来"、促进中华文化海外传播的一条可行路径。在国内外专家学者、文博机构等的支持下，新星出版社推出这套《海外藏中国艺术品》，希望能为广大读者及学者提供一套可资观赏、查阅和研究的参考读物。

《海外藏中国艺术品》出版之际，我们尤其希望通过这套书向林树中先生致敬。林树中先生自20世纪80年代起，花费近20年时间，自费走遍40多个国家和地区的200多所博物馆，呕心沥血、锲而不舍，记录了大量海外藏中国文物资料，编纂出版了《海外藏中国历代名画》，成为这一领域具有重大影响力的开创性成果。2013年，新星出版社联手林树中教授共同策划了《海外藏中国艺术品》项目，旨在全面整理他对流失海外的绘画、雕塑、书法、工艺品的丰富记录和研究成果。不幸的是，筹备工作开始不久，林树中教授因病辞世，这给整理与编纂工作带来巨大挑战，出版计划也因此被迫中断。

《海外藏中国艺术品》编纂出版的两大关键因素是专家学者的专业把关和海外藏品的图片授权。在重启并继续推动项目的过程中，我们重新组建了国内外专家组成的编纂团队，英国独角兽公司则协调许多知名博物馆向我们开放图片授权。合法取得文物图片使用授权后，编纂团队对入选文物加以鉴别与甄选，按时代顺序进行分卷、编排，并对文物中英文定名、创作时代、创作者、材质、规格等馆藏信息进行逐一确认。

《海外藏中国艺术品》共计20卷，收录文物2279件，来自海外33家知名博物馆，涵盖了铜器（2册）、陶瓷（3册）、书法（3册）、绘画（11册）和造像（1册）五大门类。

此次出版的《海外藏中国艺术品》因故未能收录金银器、玉器、服饰等艺术门类。我们愿以《海外藏中国艺术品》的出版为契机，努力搭建研究交流和成果出版发布平台，期待与国内外有关各方携手，共同推进流失文物领域相关工作，为中华优秀传统文化传承发展和中华文化国际传播作出新贡献。

囿于出版者水平，书中难免缺漏错讹之处，敬请专家、读者指正。

Preface

According to statistics from the Chinese Society of Cultural Relics, over ten million Chinese cultural relics have been dispersed overseas since the Opium War in the mid-19th century. They represent an important and unique part of China's cultural heritage. Beyond their historical, cultural, and artistic value, they are also of great interest to all sectors of society due to the national sentiments they embody.

In recent years, the Chinese government has been actively engaging in the recovery of Chinese cultural relics, and domestic and international academia has seen a surge in new research, making the study of the loss of Chinese cultural relics a burgeoning field. However, practical challenges have constrained the repatriation efforts, resulting in the recovery of only a small fraction of these relics. In light of this, it has become a feasible approach to enhance visibility and awareness of these artifacts through strengthened international cooperation, joint research, and the dissemination of materials and findings via publications and digitalization. With the support of domestic and international experts, scholars, cultural institutions, and museums, New Star Press has published the *Overseas Chinese Art Selection* series. This series aims to provide reference materials for readers and scholars to appreciate, consult, and study.

Upon the publication of this series, we would like to take this opportunity to pay tribute to Mr. Lin Shuzhong. Beginning in the 1980s, Lin devoted nearly two decades visiting over 200 museums in more than 40 countries and regions at his own expense. With remarkable dedication and perseverance, he documented a vast amount of information about Chinese cultural relics overseas and compiled and published *Famous Chinese Paintings Abroad*, which has become a groundbreaking work with significant influence in this field. In 2013, New Star Press collaborated with Professor Lin on *Overseas Chinese Art Selection*, aiming to comprehensively organize his extensive records and research on paintings, sculptures, calligraphy, and crafts lost overseas. Tragically, shortly after the preparatory work began, he passed away due to illness, presenting significant challenges to the project's continuation. As a result, the publication plan had to be suspended.

The successful compilation and publication of *Overseas Chinese Art Selection* depended on two critical factors: the professional scrutiny of experts and scholars and the license to use images granted by overseas museums. In the process of restarting the project, we set up a new compilation team composed of local and international experts. UK-based Unicorn Publishing Group LLP coordinated with many renowned overseas museums to secure permissions for image use. After legally obtaining their permissions, the compilation team appraised and selected artifacts, organized them into different categories and in chronological order, and confirmed collection information for each piece, including Chinese and English names, the time of creation, the artist's name, material, specifications, and other relevant information.

Overseas Chinese Art Selection consists of 20 volumes, with 2,279 cultural relics from 33 renowned museums overseas, covering five major categories: bronzes (two volumes), ceramics (three volumes), calligraphy (three volumes), paintings (11 volumes), and sculptures (one volume).

Categories such as gold and silver wares, jade wares, and costumes are not included. We hope this publication will help build a platform for research exchanges and publication of research findings. We are looking forward to working together with partners at home and abroad to jointly pursue initiatives related to lost Chinese cultural treasures, and contribute to the inheritance and development of China's excellent traditional culture and a wider knowledge of Chinese culture globally.

Despite our best efforts, errors and inaccuracies may be present due to the limitations of the publisher's expertise. We kindly invite experts and readers to point them out for further improvement.

凡例

一、《海外藏中国艺术品》绘画卷收录了宋、元、明、清代共1178件画作，每件画作由图片和中英文基本信息两部分组成。

二、本卷中画作依照时代分册：宋代2册，元代1册，明、清各4册，共计11册。

三、本卷中具体画作顺序基本依照画家生卒年先后编排，同时兼顾风格、流派等相关因素。同一画家的画作如有准确年款，则依年款先后编排，无准确年款的画作基本按立轴、手卷、册页、扇面形制依序编排；传为某画家的画作，均编排在该画家画作最后。佚名画作均编排于各时代最后，并依人物、山水、花鸟等门类略作分类。

四、本卷中已有中文定名的画作名称，与官网名称不一致的，均依已有中文定名。

五、本卷中以朝代标明画作的时代信息，其相应的英文表述，统一注明朝代和具体起止时间，如"Ming dynasty (1368—1644)"。部分画作有准确年款，均注明。

六、本卷中画作的材质基本统一为纸本水墨、纸本设色、绢本水墨、绢本设色、绫本水墨、绫本设色六种，对应英文为 ink on paper, ink and color on paper, ink on silk, ink and color on silk, ink on satin, ink and color on satin。将 ink and touches of color on silk；ink, color, gold and silver on silk；ink and color on gold-flecked paper；ink and pale color on paper 等统一为以上相应材质。

七、本卷中画作的尺寸基本为画面尺寸，并注明了画面纵、横尺寸，对应英文为 H、W。

八、本卷充分尊重各海外博物馆的要求，将每幅画作的出处和图片版权信息均详细列出。但因该信息并非对画作本身的描述，故未翻译成中文。其中个别博物馆或美术馆，如大阪市立美术馆，未提供该信息，因此未收录。

Guide to the Reader

i. The paintings volume of *Overseas Chinese Art Selection* contains 1178 pieces of paintings from the Song (960-1279), Yuan (1271-1368), Ming (1368-1644) and Qing (1644-1911) dynasties. Each piece is accompanied by basic information in Chinese and English.

ii. The paintings are presented chronologically in eleven volumes, of which two volumes are for paintings from Song Dynasty, one volume including those of Yuan Dynasty, four volumes for those of Ming Dynasty and another four for paintings from Qing Dynasty.

iii. The order of the paintings within each dynasty generally follows the period of time when the artists lived, taking the artistic styles, genres, etc. into consideration. Paintings by the same artist are primarily sorted in accordance with the exact chronology information when known; otherwise, they are arranged in accordance with the form of the paintings, namely in the order of handing scroll, handscroll, album leaf, fan paintings. Paintings attributed to an uncertain artist, are placed at the very end of the composer's paintings. Anonymous paintings are sorted at the end of paintings of each dynasty in this volume in accordance with the category of figure, scenery, birds and flowers, etc.

iv. The established Chinese names of those paintings which may be given different names by the official website will be retained in this volume.

v. The era of the paintings is marked by the dynasty in the volume. Both the dynasty and specific starting and ending years of the dynasties are indicated in the English description, such as "Ming Dynasty (1368-1644)". The specific creating time of some paintings is already known, which has been presented clearly.

vi. The materials used in the paintings in this volume are primarily summarized into six types: namely ink on paper, ink and color on paper, ink on silk, ink and color on silk, ink on stain, ink and color on stain. While there are numerous varitions, such as ink and touches of color on silk; ink, color, gold and silver on silk; ink and color on gold-flecked paper; ink and pale color on paper; etc. These have been standardized to the above categories for consistency.

vii. Dimensions in the basic information of this volume primarily represent the size of the painting's image, with vertical measurements denoted by 'H' and horizontal measurements by 'W'.

viii. This volume fully respects the requirements of overseas museums, the credit line and image copyright of paintings provided by the museums have been listed in details. However, since such information is not a description of the paintings themselves, it is presented only in English. Some museums or galleries, such as The Osaka City Museum of Fine Arts, do not provide those information of the paintings when displaying them, therefore such information of some paintings is omitted here.

目 录
CONTENTS

宋（下）
The Song Dynasty（2）

78. 山市晴岚图 003
Mountain Market and Clearing Mist

79. 湖畔幽居图 005
Retirement by Side of Lake

80. 残阳渔村图 006
Fishing Village in Twilight Glow

81. 山水图 007
Landscape

82. 山水图 008
Landscape

83. 泽畔急风图 009
Windswept Lakeshore

84. 长臂猿图 010
Swinging Gibbon

85. 释迦出山图 011
Sakyamuni Descending Mountain After Asceticism

86. 太白吟行图 012
Li Bai in Stroll

87. 六祖截竹图 013
Sixth Patriarch Cutting Bamboo

88. 雪景山水图 014
Snowscape

89. 泽畔行吟图 015
Poet Strolling by Lakeshore

90. 寒禽图 016
Winter Birds

91. 芦苇水禽图 017
Waterfowl and Reeds

92. 龙虎图 019
Dragon and Tiger

93. 叭叭鸟图 020
Myna

94. 荷燕图 021
Swallow and Lotus

95. 水月观音图 022
White-robed Bodhisattva Avalokitesvara

96. 牧牛图 023
Man, Buffalo and Calf

97. 胡骑春猎图 024
Nomads Hunting with Falcons

98. 胡骑秋猎图 025
Autumn Hunt

99. 吉祥多子图 026
Orange, Grapes and Pomegranates

100. 雾江舟行图 027
Full Sail on Misty River

101. 猿图 028
Monkey

102. 喜鹊双兔图 029
Magpies and Wild Rabbits

103. 五龙图 031
Five Dragons

104. 竹鸡图 032
Cockerel and Bamboo

105. 雏雀图 033
Sparrows Chicks in Basket

106. 松下高士图 034
Landscape with Great Pine

107. 春郊回雁图 035
Landscape with Flying Geese

108. 坐看云起图 036
Scholar Reclining and Watching Rising Clouds

I

| 109. 兰花图 037
Orchids | 129. 白衣观音坐像 068
White-robed Budhisattva Avalokitesvara on Rock |
|---|---|
| 110. 鱼乐图 039
Pleasures of Fishes | 130. 普贤菩萨像 069
Samantabhadra |
| 111. 水仙图 043
Narcissus | 131. 文殊菩萨像 070
Manjusri on Lion with Attendant |
| 112. 骏骨图 046
Emaciated Horse | 132. 阿弥陀佛与胁侍菩萨像 071
Buddha Amitabha with Two Attending Bodhisattvas |
| 113. 墨兰图 047
Ink Orchid | 133. 达摩面壁图 072
Bodhidharma Meditating Facing Cliff |
| 114. 送郝玄明使秦图 049
Farewell to Hao Xuanming Envoy | 134. 十六罗汉像 073
Sixteen Arhats |
| 115. 罗汉浣衣图 050
Luohan Laudering | 135. 罗汉坐像 074
Seated Arhat with Two Attendants |
| 116. 天台石桥图 051
Rock Bridge at Mount Tiantai | 136. 静坐罗汉像 075
Fifth Luohan Nakula |
| 117. 十王图之一 052
Ten Kings of Hell | 137. 佛道主题画册（选十）......077
Album of Daoist and Buddhist Themes |
| 118. 十王图之二 053
Ten Kings of Hell | 138. 洞天论道图 079
Conversation in Cave |
| 119. 十王图之三 054
Ten Kings of Hell | 139. 挑耳图 081
Library Scene |
| 120. 十王图之四 055
Ten Kings of Hell | 140. 吕洞宾过岳阳楼图 083
Immortal Lv Dongbin Appearing over Yueyang Pavilion |
| 121. 十王图之五 056
Ten Kings of Hell | 141. 射雁图 084
Three Horsemen Hunting Wild Geese |
| 122. 十六罗汉图 057
Sixteen Arhats | 142. 樵夫归家图 085
Woodcutters Returning Home |
| 123. 妙法莲华经之观世音菩萨像 062
Avalokitesvara Bodhisattva | 143. 狸奴婴戏图 086
Child with his Pets in Flower Garden |
| 124. 释迦出山图 063
Sakyamuni Emerging from Mountains | 144. 牧牛图 087
Cowherd from Album of Old Master Paintings |
| 125. 阿弥陀佛像 064
Buddha Amitabha Descending from His Pure Land | 145. 牧牛图 088
Herd-boy Mounting Water Buffalo |
| 126. 阿弥陀佛像 065
Buddha Amitabha Descending from his Pure Land | 146. 骑驴图 089
Chan Master Riding Mule |
| 127. 阿弥陀佛图 066
Amitabha Trinity Descending on Clouds | 147. 归去来兮辞图 091
Illustrations to Tao Qian's Prose Poem "Homecoming" |
| 128. 观音像 067
Bodhisattva Avalokitesvara and Immortal Shancai Crossing Sea | 148. 庞灵照图 094
Snowscape with Standing Woman |

149. 草堂对坐图 ....095 Conversation in Thatched Hut	169. 山村策杖图 ....126 Retired Scholar Enjoying Mountain Scenery
150. 田家风俗图 ....097 Peasants Moving	170. 雪山行旅图 ....127 Travelers in Snowy Mountains
151. 明皇幸蜀图 ....099 Emperor Xuanzong's Flight to Shu	171. 夜潮图 ....128 Waves in Moonlight
152. 仙山楼阁图 ....100 Palace Landscape	172. 冬景图 ....129 Winter Landscape
153. 仿范宽山水图 ....101 Landscape After Fan Kuan	173. 观瀑图 ....130 Watching Waterfall
154. 溪山无尽图 ....103 Streams and Mountains Without End	174. 柳荫策杖图 ....132 Sage and Attendant Beneath Willow
155. 别苑春山图 ....107 Retreats in Spring Hills	175. 湖畔庭院图 ....133 Strolling to Lakeside Gazebo
156. 泛舟柳塘图 ....108 Boating by Willow Bank	176. 蜀江图 ....135 Shu River
157. 江行图 ....109 Boats at Anchor	177. 观瀑图 ....138 Watching Waterfall
158. 长江万里图 ....111 Ten Thousand Li Along Yangzi River	178. 风雨归舟图 ....139 Returning Boat in Wind and Rain
159. 渡津图 ....116 Waiting for Ferry	179. 山水图 ....140 Landscape
160. 桃花春水图 ....117 Peach Blossoms by Spring River	180. 幽禽寒林图 ....141 Two Birds on Wintry Tree
161. 岸边柳树图 ....118 Willows	181. 雪江待渡图 ....142 Waiting for Ferry
162. 雪桥送别图 ....119 Bridge in Snow	182. 冒雨寻庄图 ....143 Returning Home in Driving Rain
163. 归舟图 ....120 Towing Boat in Rainstorm	183. 春山图 ....144 Early Spring Landscape
164. 雪景图 ....121 Winter Scene	184. 江行图 ....145 Voyage Along the River
165. 坐观云雾图 ....122 Misty Landscape with Scholars and Attendants	185. 古柏归禽图 ....146 Returning Birds and Old Cypress
166. 观瀑图 ....123 Viewing Waterfall	186. 花鸟图 ....147 Flower and Bird
167. 秋江渔艇图 ....124 Fishing Boats on Autumn River	187. 梅花幽鸟图 ....148 Bird on Flowering Branch
168. 渔舟图 ....125 Fishing Boat	188. 桃枝双鸟图 ....149 Birds on Peach Branch

189. 梅竹雀鸟图 .... 150 Sparrows Plum Blossoms and Bamboo	203. 玉兰栖禽图 .... 164 Bird on Flowering Branch
190. 三猿得鹭图 .... 151 Gibbons Raiding Egret's Nest	204. 寒林归鸦图 .... 165 Flock of Birds Returning to Wintry Woods
191. 芦塘鸥鹭图 .... 152 Egrets in Water Reeds	205. 莲池水禽图 .... 167 Lotus Pond and Waterfowl
192. 牧牛图 .... 153 Water Buffalo, Calf and Herdboy	206. 墨竹图 .... 168 Ink Bamboo
193. 观梅图 .... 154 Scholar Admiring Plum Blossoms	207. 枇杷八哥图 .... 169 Minah Bird on Loquat Branch
194. 红芍药图 .... 155 Peony Flower and Leaves	208. 犬图 .... 170 Dog Watching
195. 腊梅图 .... 156 Snow Plum	209. 斗牛图 .... 171 Two Fighting Water Buffaloes
196. 鼠食荔枝图 .... 157 Mouse Eating Lichee Fruit	210. 竹虫图 .... 172 Insects and Bamboo
197. 秋瓜图 .... 158 Squash	211. 猿鹿图 .... 173 Gibbons and Deer
198. 雪雁图 .... 159 Wild Geese in Winter	212. 百牛图 .... 175 One Hundred Water Buffalo
199. 秋岸水鸟图 .... 160 Birds on Autumn Inlet	213. 仙驭奇禽图 .... 176 Immortal Riding Dragon
200. 水仙图 ....161 Narcissus	版权支持 .... 177 Image Contributors
201. 竹石图 .... 162 Bamboo Landscape	编辑、出版人员 .... 179 Editorial Staff
202. 雪岸寒鸦图 .... 163 Birds and Ducks on Snowy Islet	

宋（下）

The Song Dynasty (2)

78. 山市晴岚图

南宋
夏圭
绢本水墨
册页
纵24.8、横21.3厘米
大都会艺术博物馆

Mountain Market and Clearing Mist

Southern Song dynasty (1127–1279)
Xia Gui
Ink on silk
Album leaf
H×W : 24.8×21.3 cm
The Metropolitan Museum of Art
John Stewart Kennedy Fund, 1913

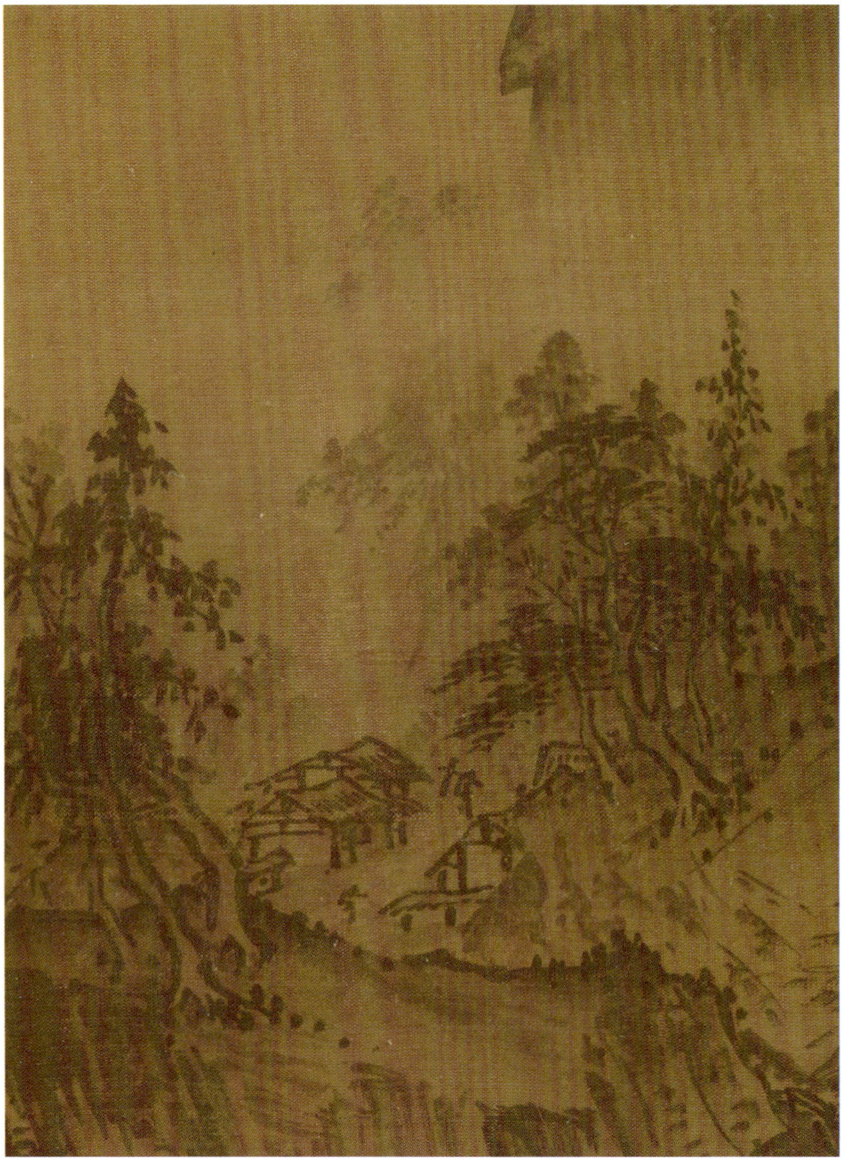

79. 湖畔幽居图

南宋
夏圭
绢本设色
册页
纵25.2、横25.9厘米
大阪市立美术馆

Retirement by Side of Lake

Southern Song dynasty (1127–1279)
Xia Gui
Ink and color on silk
Album leaf
H×W : 25.2×25.9 cm
The Osaka City Museum of Fine Arts

80. 残阳渔村图

南宋
（传）夏圭
绢本设色
册页
纵33.02厘米
印第安纳波利斯艺术博物馆

Fishing Village in Twilight Glow

Southern Song dynasty (1127–1279)
Attributed to Xia Gui
Ink and color on silk
Album leaf
H: 33.02cm
The Indianapolis Museum of Art
Gift of Mr. and Mrs. Eli Lilly

81. 山水图

南宋
（传）夏圭
绢本水墨
册页
纵22.5、横25.4厘米
东京国立博物馆

Landscape

Southern Song dynasty (1127–1279)
Attributed to Xia Gui
Ink on silk
Album leaf
H×W : 22.5×25.4 cm
The Tokyo National Museum
ColBase(https://colbase.nich.go.jp/collection_items/tnm/TA-339?locale=ja)

82. 山水图

南宋
（传）夏圭
绢本水墨
册页
纵25.9、横34.3厘米
东京国立博物馆

Landscape

Southern Song dynasty (1127–1279)
Attributed to Xia Gui
Ink on silk
Album leaf
H×W : 25.9×34.3 cm
The Tokyo National Museum
ColBase(https://colbase.nich.go.jp/collection_items/tnm/TA-344?locale=ja)

83. 泽畔急风图

南宋
（传）夏圭
绢本水墨
册页
纵26、横27厘米
大都会艺术博物馆

Windswept Lakeshore

Southern Song dynasty (1127–1279)
Attributed to Xia Gui
Ink on silk
Album leaf
H×W : 26×27 cm
The Metropolitan Museum of Art
Ex coll.: C. C. Wang Family, Purchase, Theodore M. Davis Collection, Bequest of Theodore M. Davis, by exchange, 1973

84. 长臂猿图

南宋
（传）夏圭
绢本设色
册页
纵24.8、横26.5厘米
克利夫兰美术馆

Swinging Gibbon

Southern Song dynasty (1127–1279)
Attributed to Xia Gui
Ink and color on silk
Album leaf
H×W : 24.8×26.5 cm
The Cleveland Museum of Art
John L. Severance Fund 1978.1

85. 释迦出山图   **Sakyamuni Descending Mountain After Asceticism**

南宋淳祐四年（公元1244年）
梁楷
绢本设色
立轴
纵118.4、横52厘米
东京国立博物馆

Southern Song dynasty (1127–1279), dated 1244
Liang Kai
Ink and color on silk
Hanging scroll
H×W : 118.4×52 cm
The Tokyo National Museum
ColBase(https://colbase.nich.go.jp/collection_items/tnm/TA-617?locale=ja)

86. 太白吟行图

南宋
梁楷
纸本水墨
立轴
纵81.1、横30.5厘米
东京国立博物馆

Li Bai in Stroll

Southern Song dynasty (1127–1279)
Liang Kai
Ink on paper
Hanging scroll
H×W : 81.1×30.5 cm
The Tokyo National Museum
ColBase(https://colbase.nich.go.jp/collection_items/tnm/TA-164?locale=ja)

87. 六祖截竹图

南宋
梁楷
纸本水墨
立轴
纵72.7、横31.5厘米
东京国立博物馆

Sixth Patriarch Cutting Bamboo

Southern Song dynasty (1127–1279)
Liang Kai
Ink on paper
Hanging scroll
H×W : 72.7×31.5 cm
The Tokyo National Museum
ColBase(https://colbase.nich.go.jp/collection_items/tnm/TA-143?locale=ja)

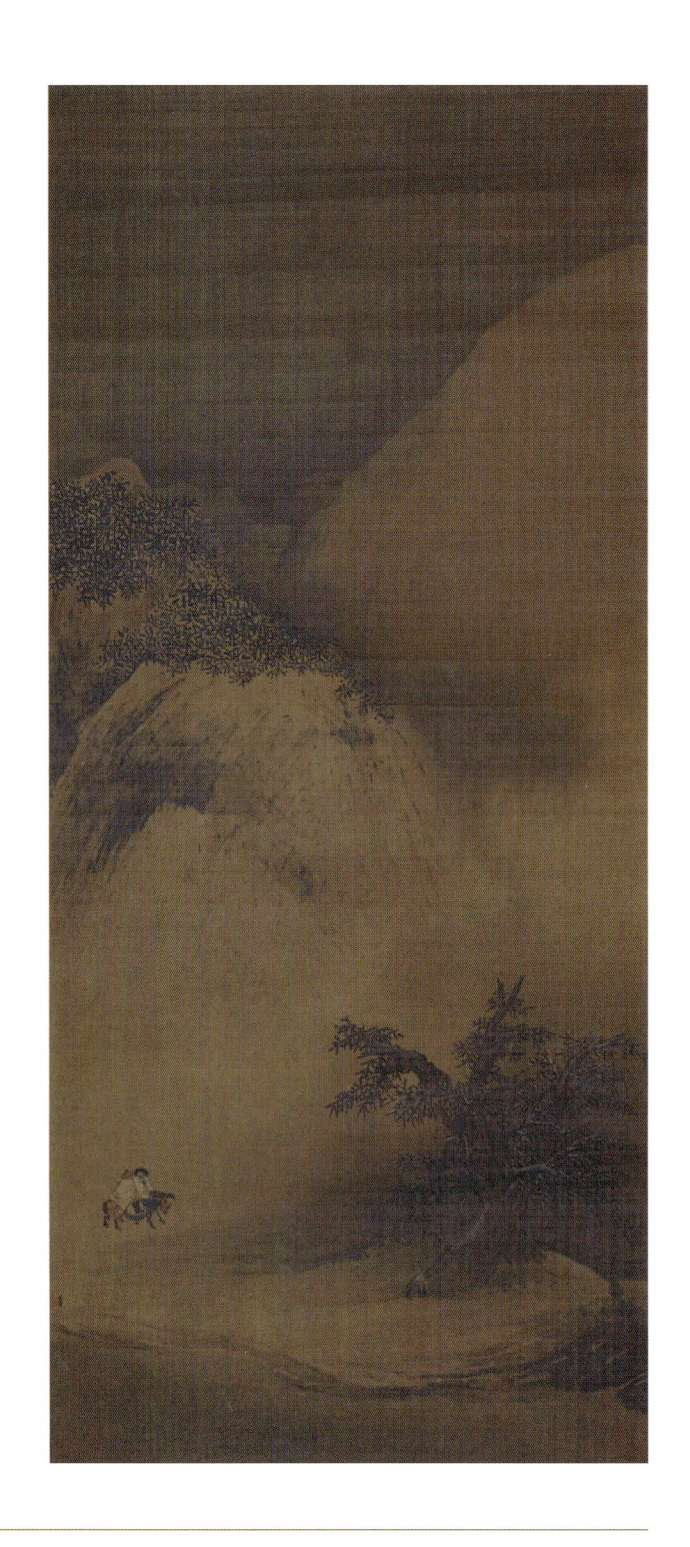

88. 雪景山水图

南宋
梁楷
绢本设色
立轴
纵110.3、横49.7厘米
东京国立博物馆

Snowscape

Southern Song dynasty (1127–1279)
Liang Kai
Ink and color on silk
Hanging scroll
H×W : 110.3×49.7 cm
The Tokyo National Museum
ColBase(https://colbase.nich.go.jp/collection_items/tnm/TA-326?locale=ja)

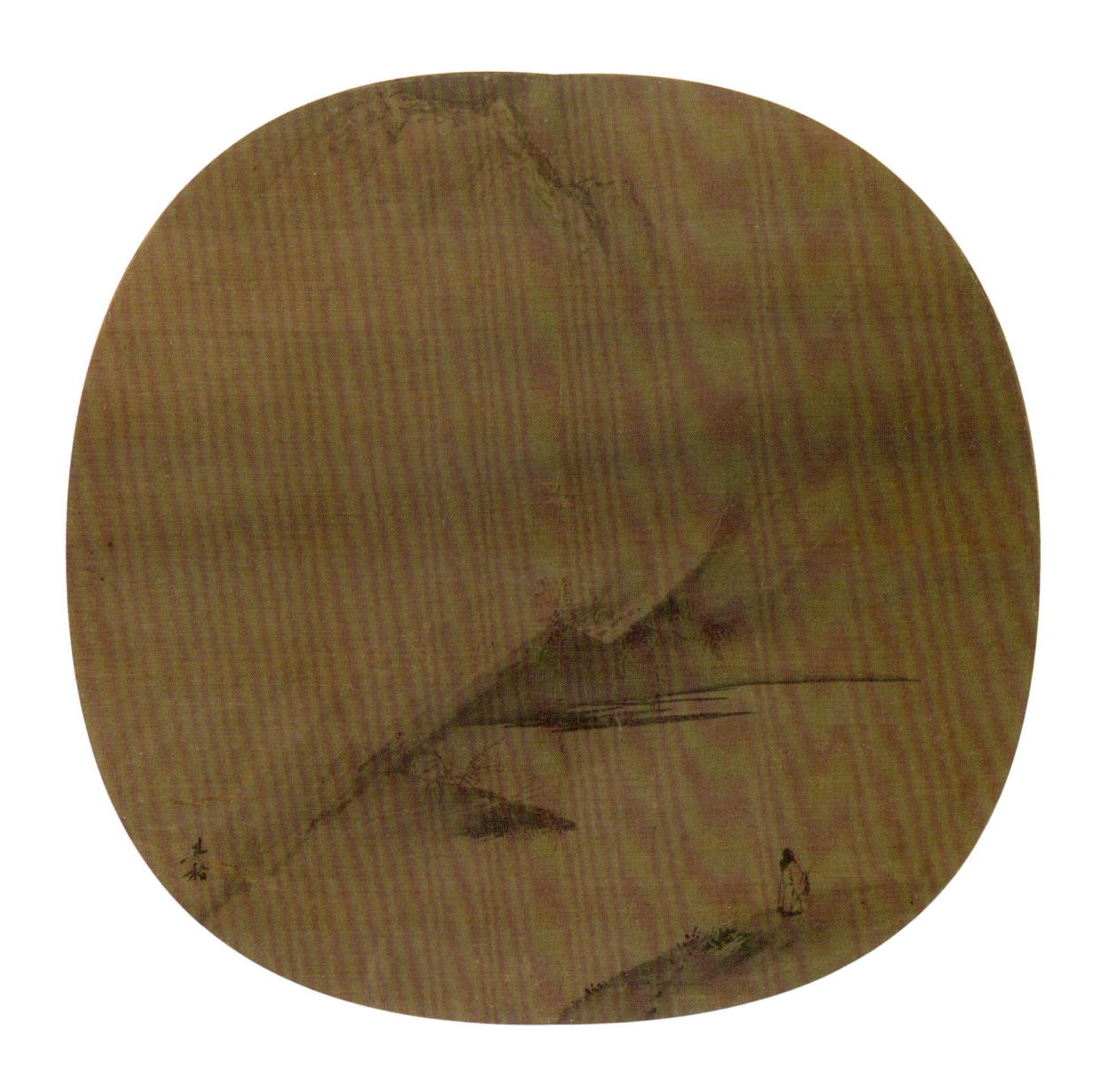

89. 泽畔行吟图

南宋
梁楷
绢本水墨
册页
纵22.9、横24.3厘米
大都会艺术博物馆

Poet Strolling by Lakeshore

Southern Song dynasty (1127–1279)
Liang Kai
Ink on silk
Album leaf
H×W : 22.9×24.3 cm
The Metropolitan Museum of Art
Bequest of John M. Crawford Jr., 1988

90. 寒禽图

南宋
梁楷
绢本设色
册页
纵24.6、横25.4厘米
哈佛艺术博物馆

Winter Birds

Southern Song dynasty (1127–1279)
Liang Kai
Ink and color on silk
Album leaf
H×W : 24.6×25.4 cm
The Harvard Art Museums
© President and Fellows of Harvard College

91. 芦苇水禽图

南宋
（传）梁楷
绢本水墨
册页
纵23、横22.9厘米
克利夫兰美术馆

Waterfowl and Reeds

Southern Song dynasty (1127–1279)
Attributed to Liang Kai
Ink on silk
Album leaf
H×W : 23×22.9 cm
The Cleveland Museum of Art
Leonard C. Hanna, Jr. Fund 1984.42

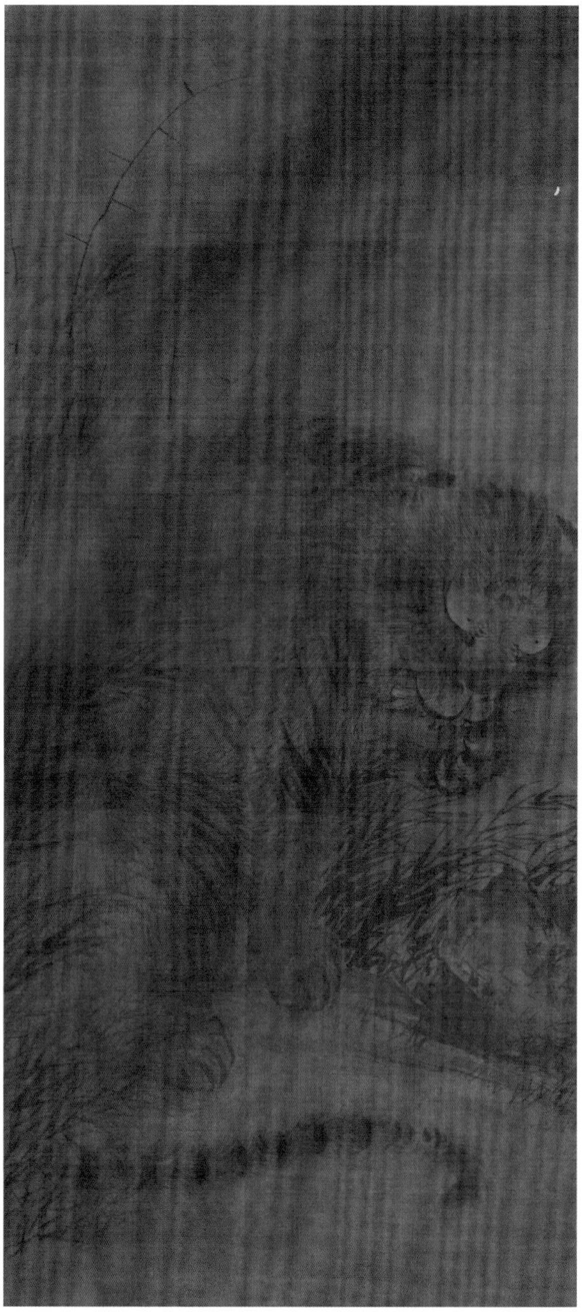

92. 龙虎图

南宋
牧溪
绢本水墨
立轴
纵123.8、横55.9厘米
克利夫兰美术馆

Dragon and Tiger

Southern Song dynasty (1127–1279)
Mu Xi
Ink on silk
Hanging scroll
H×W : 123.8×55.9 cm
The Cleveland Museum of Art
Purchase from the J. H. Wade Fund 1958.427

93. 叭叭鸟图

南宋
（传）牧溪
纸本水墨
立轴
纵60.4、横30.9厘米
克利夫兰美术馆

Myna

Southern Song dynasty (1127–1279)
Attributed to Mu Xi
Ink on paper
Hanging scroll
H×W : 60.4×30.9 cm
The Cleveland Museum of Art
John L. Severance Fund 1982.53

94. 荷燕图

南宋
（传）牧溪
绢本水墨
立轴
纵91.8、横47厘米
克利夫兰美术馆

Swallow and Lotus

Southern Song dynasty (1127–1279)
Attributed to Mu Xi
Ink on silk
Hanging scroll
H×W : 91.8×47 cm
The Cleveland Museum of Art
Purchase from the J. H. Wade Fund 1981.34

95. 水月观音图

宋或元
（传）张月壶
纸本水墨
立轴
纵104、横42.3厘米
克利夫兰美术馆

White-robed Bodhisattva Avalokitesvara

Song dynasty (960–1279) or Yuan dynasty (1271–1368)
Attributed to Zhang Yuehu
Ink on paper
Hanging scroll
H×W : 104×42.3 cm
The Cleveland Museum of Art
Leonard C. Hanna, Jr. Fund 1972.160

96. 牧牛图

南宋
李祐
绢本设色
册页
纵25、横26.7厘米
克利夫兰美术馆

Man, Buffalo and Calf

Southern Song dynasty (1127–1279)
Li You
Ink and color on silk
Album leaf
H×W : 25×26.7 cm
The Cleveland Museum of Art
Severance and Greta Millikin Purchase Fund
1960.41

97. 胡骑春猎图

南宋
（传）陈居中
绢本设色
册页
纵24.1、横27.3厘米
大都会艺术博物馆

Nomads Hunting with Falcons

Southern Song dynasty (1127–1279)
Attributed to Chen Juzhong
Ink and color on silk
Album leaf
H×W : 24.1×27.3 cm
The Metropolitan Museum of Art
From the Collection of A. W. Bahr,
Purchase, Fletcher Fund, 1947

98. 胡骑秋猎图

南宋
（传）陈居中
绢本设色
册页
纵24.4、横27.3厘米
克利夫兰美术馆

Autumn Hunt

Southern Song dynasty (1127–1279)
Attributed to Chen Juzhong
Ink and color on silk
Album leaf
H×W : 24.4×27.3 cm
The Cleveland Museum of Art
Charles W. Harkness Endowment Fund
1930.314

99. 吉祥多子图

南宋
（传）鲁宗贵
绢本设色
册页
纵24、横25.8厘米
波士顿艺术博物馆

Orange, Grapes and Pomegranates

Southern Song dynasty (1127–1279)
Attributed to Lu Zonggui
Ink and color on silk
Album leaf
H×W : 24×25.8 cm
The Museum of Fine Arts, Boston
Bequest of Charles Bain Hoyt–Charles Bain Hoyt Collection
© 2024 Museum of Fine Arts, Boston

100. 雾江舟行图

南宋
夏生
绢本水墨
团扇
纵24.2、横26.1厘米
克利夫兰美术馆

Full Sail on Misty River

Southern Song dynasty (1127–1279)
Xia Sheng
Ink on silk
Round fan
H×W : 24.2×26.1 cm
The Cleveland Museum of Art
Bequest of Mrs. A. Dean Perry 1997.90

101. 猿图

南宋
（传）毛松
绢本设色
册页
纵47、横36.5厘米
东京国立博物馆

Monkey

Southern Song dynasty (1127–1279)
Attributed to Mao Song
Ink and color on silk
Album leaf
H×W : 47×36.5 cm
The Tokyo National Museum
ColBase(https://colbase.nich.go.jp/collection_items/tnm/TA-297?locale=ja)

102. 喜鹊双兔图

南宋
李永
绢本设色
册页
纵25、横24.5厘米
克利夫兰美术馆

Magpies and Wild Rabbits

Southern Song dynasty (1127–1279)
Li Yong
Ink and color on silk
Album leaf
H×W : 25×24.5 cm
The Cleveland Museum of Art
Bequest of Mrs. A. Dean Perry 1997.87

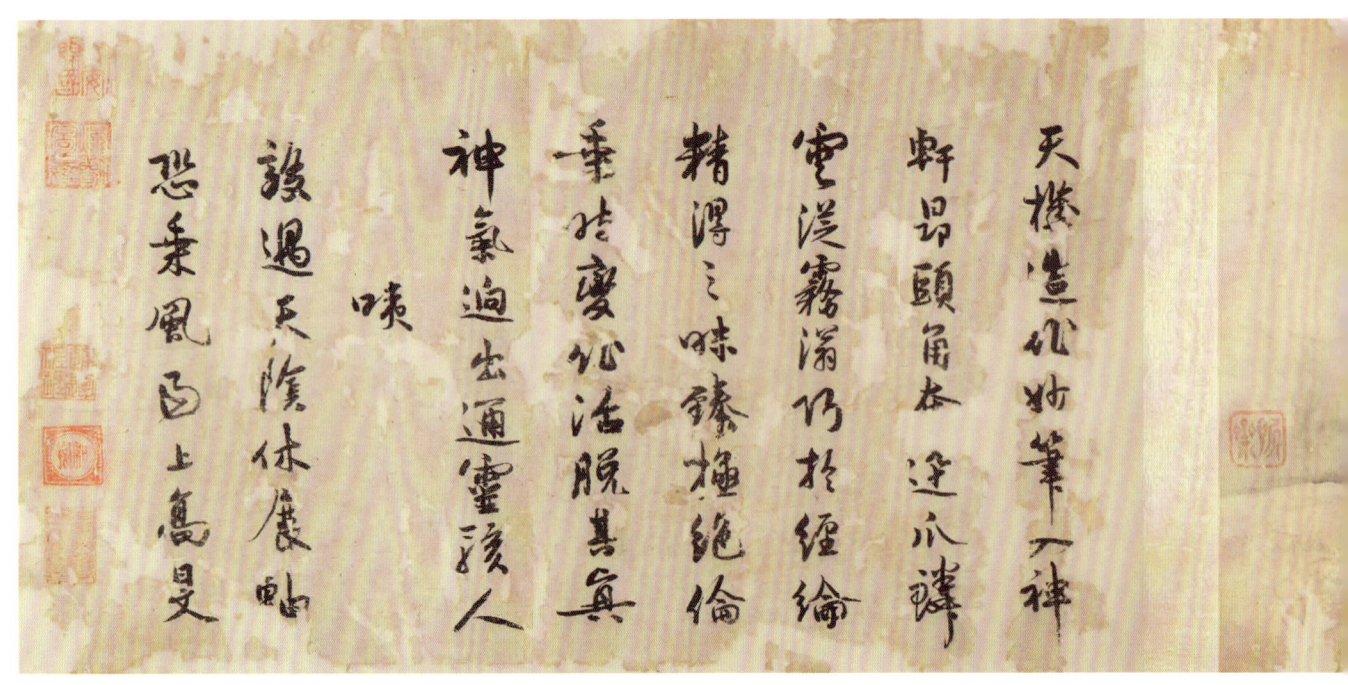

天機造化妙筆入神
軒昂頭角本遂爪髯
電送霧滃巧於經綸
精浮之昧臻極絕倫
乘時變化活脫甚真
神氣逈出通靈駭人
噫
譎遇天陰休展眇
恐乘風雨上高旻

103. 五龙图

南宋
（传）陈容
纸本设色
手卷
纵45.2、横299.5厘米
东京国立博物馆

Five Dragons

Southern Song dynasty (1127–1279)
Attributed to Chen Rong
Ink and color on paper
Handscroll
H×W : 45.2×299.5 cm
The Tokyo National Museum
ColBase(https://colbase.nich.go.jp/collection_items/tnm/TA-363?locale=ja)

104. 竹鸡图

南宋
萝窗
绢本设色
立轴
纵96.3、横43.4厘米
东京国立博物馆

Cockerel and Bamboo

Southern Song dynasty (1127–1279)
Luo Chuang
Ink and color on silk
Hanging scroll
H×W : 96.3×43.4 cm
The Tokyo National Museum
ColBase(https://colbase.nich.go.jp/collection_items/tnm/TA-341?locale=ja)

105. 雏雀图

南宋
（传）宋汝志
绢本设色
册页
纵21.7、横22.5厘米
东京国立博物馆

Sparrows Chicks in Basket

Southern Song dynasty (1127–1279)
Attributed to Song Ruzhi
Ink and color on silk
Album leaf
H×W : 21.7×22.5 cm
The Tokyo National Museum
ColBase(https://colbase.nich.go.jp/collection_items/tnm/TA-355?locale=ja)

106. 松下高士图

南宋
马麟
绢本设色
册页
纵25.2、横26厘米
大都会艺术博物馆

Landscape with Great Pine

Southern Song dynasty (1127–1279)
Ma Lin
Ink and color on silk
Album leaf
H×W : 25.2×26 cm
The Metropolitan Museum of Art
From the Collection of A. W. Bahr, Purchase, Fletcher Fund, 1947

107. 春郊回雁图

南宋
马麟
绢本设色
册页
纵25.5、横26.5厘米
克利夫兰美术馆

Landscape with Flying Geese

Southern Song dynasty (1127–1279)
Ma Lin
Ink and color on silk
Album leaf
H×W : 25.5×26.5 cm
The Cleveland Museum of Art
John L. Severance Fund 1952.285

108. 坐看云起图

南宋
马麟
绢本水墨
册页
纵25.1、横25.3厘米
克利夫兰美术馆

Scholar Reclining and Watching Rising Clouds

Southern Song dynasty (1127–1279)
Ma Lin
Ink on silk
Album leaf
H×W : 25.1×25.3 cm
The Cleveland Museum of Art
John L. Severance Fund 1961.421

109. 兰花图

南宋
（传）马麟
绢本设色
册页
纵26.5、横22.5厘米
大都会艺术博物馆

Orchids

Southern Song dynasty (1127–1279)
Attributed to Ma Lin
Ink and color on silk
Album leaf
H×W : 26.5×22.5 cm
The Metropolitan Museum of Art
Ex coll.: C. C. Wang Family, Gift of The Dillon Fund, 1973

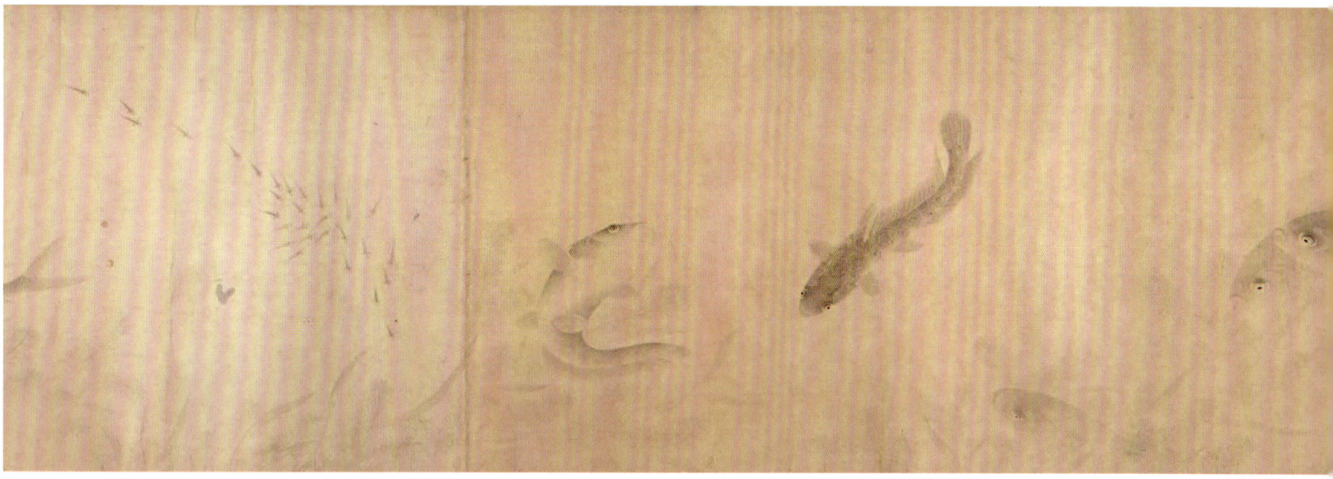

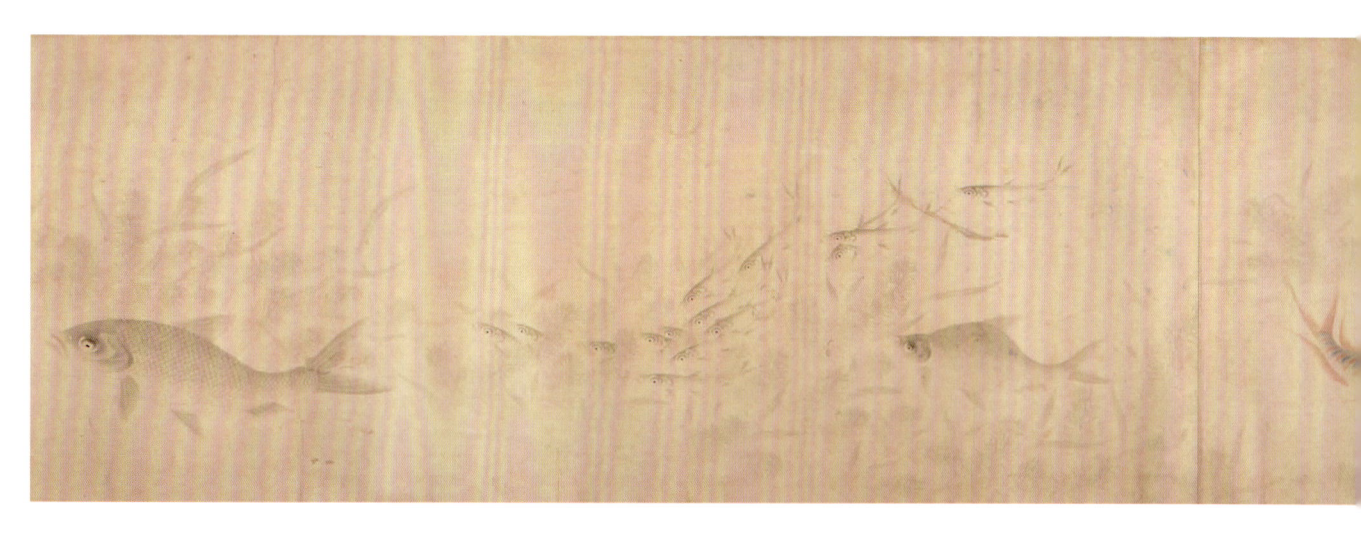

110. 鱼乐图

宋或元
（传）周东卿
纸本设色
手卷
纵30.8、横593.7厘米
大都会艺术博物馆

Pleasures of Fishes

Song dynasty (960–1279) or Yuan dynasty (1271–1368)
Attributed to Zhou Dongqing
Ink and color on paper
Handscroll
H×W : 30.8×593.7 cm
The Metropolitan Museum of Art
From the Collection of A. W. Bahr, Purchase, Fletcher Fund, 1947

非魚豈知樂
寓意寫成圖
數探申庸奧
分明有象徵
至元辛卯春仲
臨江周東鄉作

文信國題周東鄉畫魚詩
玉觀君瀟灑湘國起哀
懷古心周在宋末即以畫
名此圖作於至元辛卯乃
世祖廿八年其人王元初尚
在也　濠上誤書據古
信國辛於至元十九年至乙卯以為
至信國辛後九年再作西題
東鄉畫魚詩乃別考名此卷
如於昨見東如此與為晚年
所作矣其自題一作於濠上更
有悟入云
道光丙申九月吳榮光記

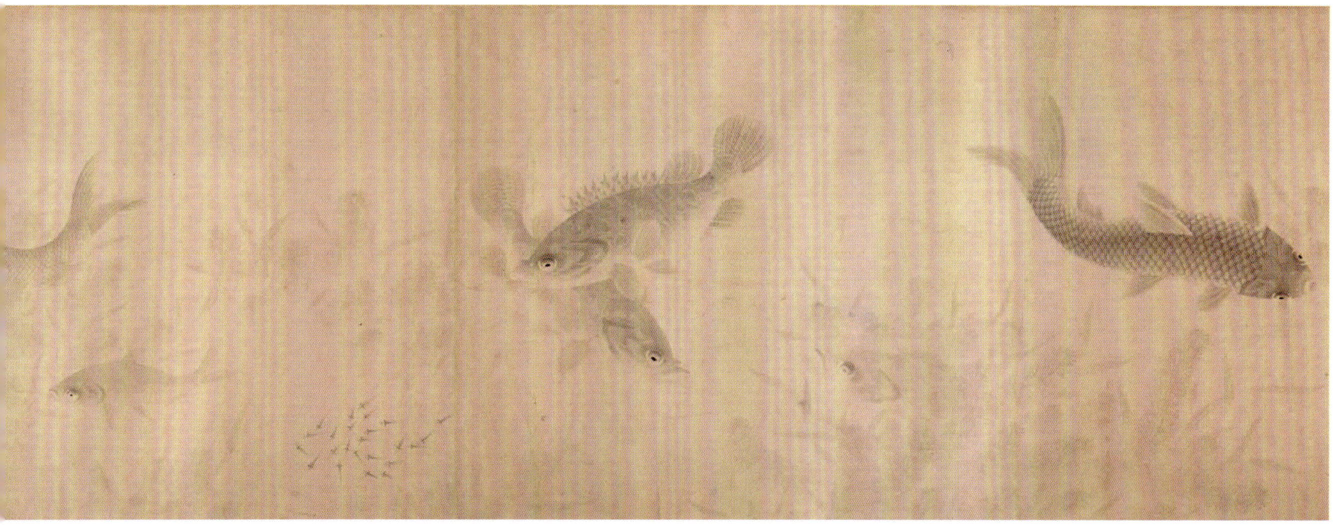

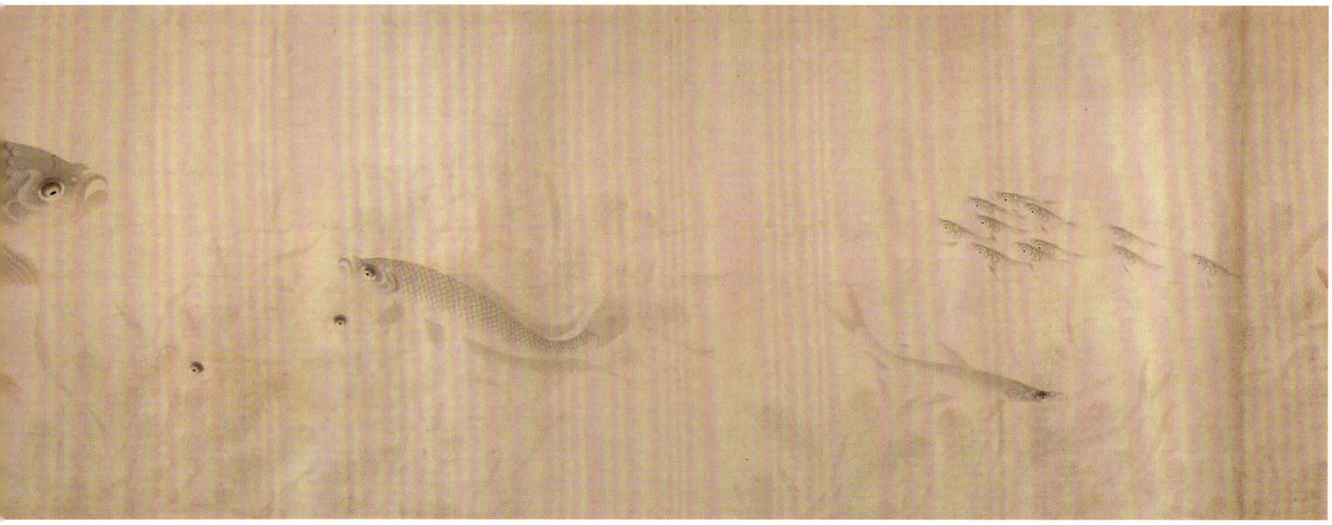

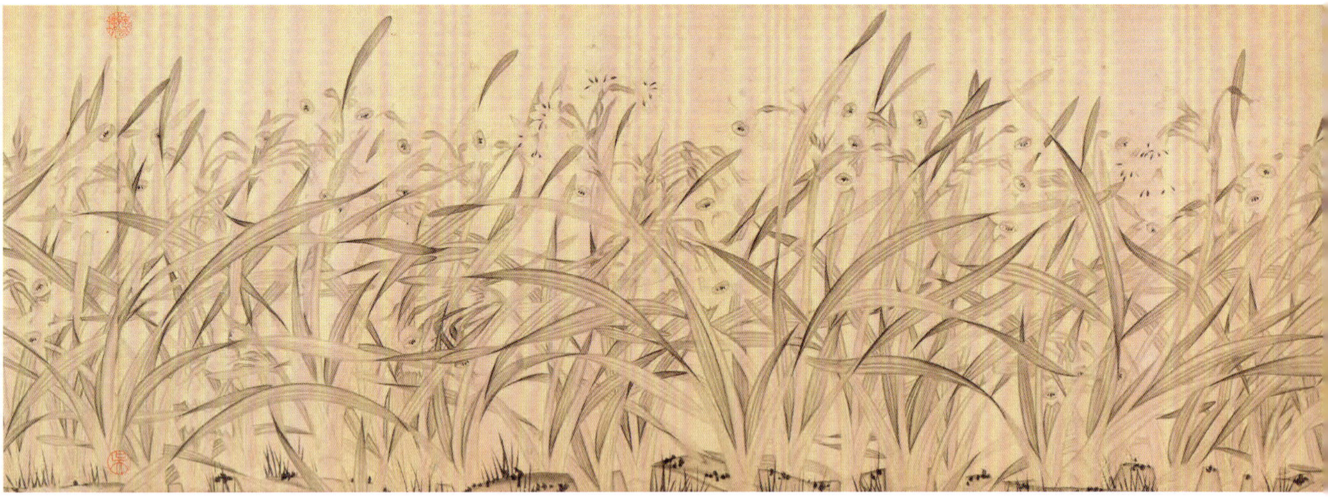

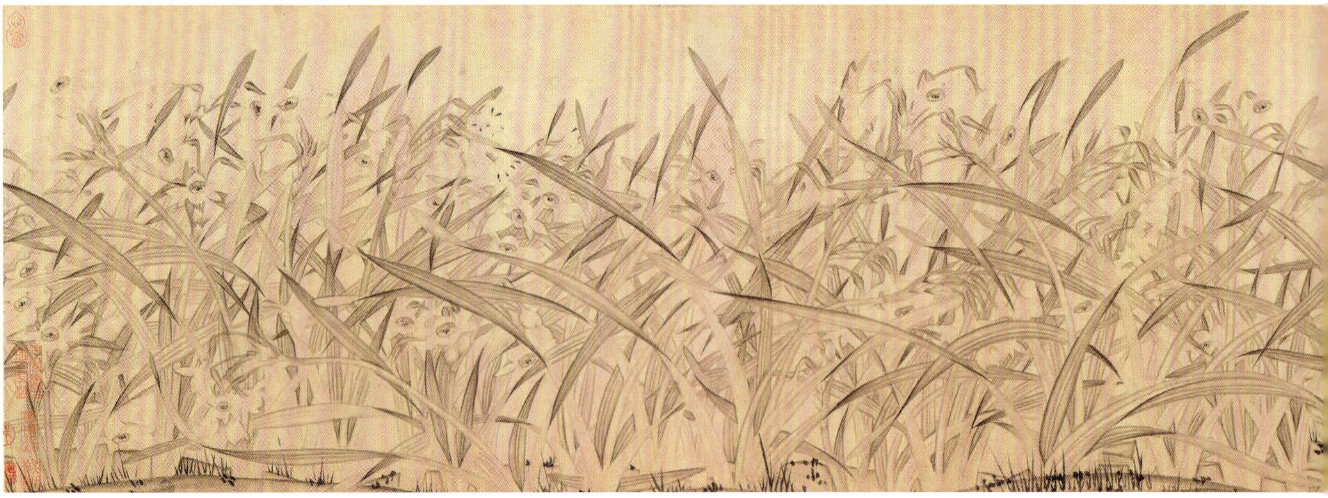

111. 水仙图

南宋
赵孟坚
纸本水墨
手卷
纵33.2、横374厘米
大都会艺术博物馆

Narcissus

Southern Song dynasty (1127–1279)
Zhao Mengjian
Ink on paper
Handscroll
H×W: 33.2×374 cm
The Metropolitan Museum of Art
Ex coll.: C. C. Wang Family, Gift of The Dillon Fund, 1973

秋觀九畹畫白鷺鷥傾流
瀅青明寶玦碎珊瑚卻憐不
得同蘭蕙一識清醒楚大夫
　　　　　　西湖仇遠

水仙花前人畫者罕見嘗見平原公子
之筆清而踈甚可愛也今此卷蘙而不
俗尤覺可觀蓋踈則易清繁則易俗
然則此作其可草〻觀耶
　　　　　　東吳林鍾

水精宮闕半不閒儔子出遊
凌素波何事伍頭卬的月不
知雲露濕衣多　天台李至剛

瀅懷低欵俯俛葉蕊皆不弱然
用墨用筆〻精妙此宋以後畫家所無
措手詢菇苑之奇珍此後有周公謹題
國香慢詞〻即紈扇好詞四至宗戎
有書體方整精健得傳本神髓興
草窔韻語字蹟如出一手當是其晚
歲所書後邨齊周密〻印及周公
藝氏寓王印仿隸篆乃周王子孫學
其下有仇山邨七絕三首押山邨遺
民印仇山村左元初隱居於邑所居
左邑東之仇山即元初房山故園者
邨李昂贊同係後先歇欵鄧
文原詩張渶題劉第題記張伯淳詩
尚是清初為粼大割裂而茅岡山
邨遠蹟幸存而殊吳此先薦
藏元和到子山家後屬友書其直
拱遇雲樓書查記咸即以考兩貝
直〻後毅孫共兒〻季值擕得
之攜以見示并屬補詠贈朱二詞
牡門靜酌句幸眼福不淺也
丙子年閏青餘杭褚德彝記

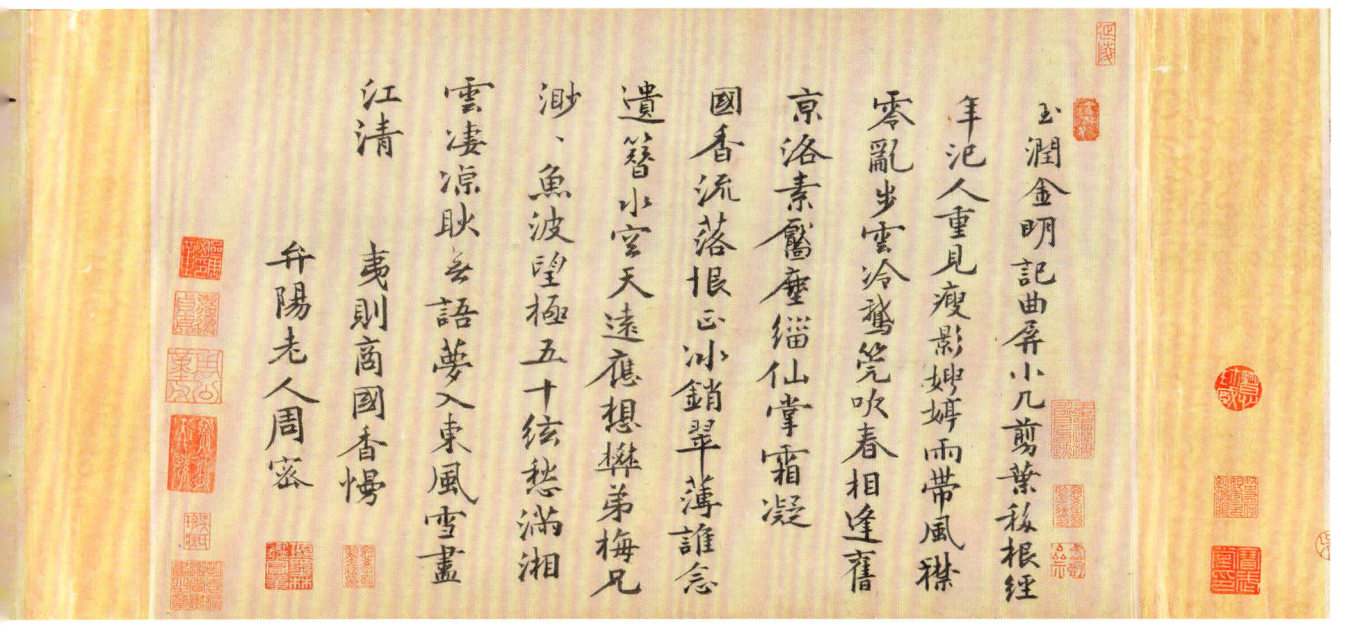

玉潤金明記曲屏小几翦葉栽根經
年沼人重見瘦影娉婷帶風襟
零亂步雲冷鶯笑吹春相逢舊
京洛素靨塵緇仙掌霜凝
國香流落恨正冰銷翠薄誰念
遺簪小宮天遠應想棣弟梅兄
渺、魚波望極五十絃愁滿湘
江清　夷則商國香慢
雲淒涼耿忘語夢入東風雪盡
　　　　　　弁陽老人周密

僝骨珊々擁湘皋玉佩漢嚴銅槃相逢
縞衣羅帶願花妍只怨王孫芳州軌
蔬子感要天寒無言自於籠淚單黃金腰
鮮青珊　多應身藏便雲茶未沐秀
色誰餐競姑肌雪空尚煙霧乘鸞却淺
銀河笙脆和䃜蘆吹散人間傷心興終古
隆吉冬青思肖秋蘭
　　　自題子固凌波圖卷同賦韻
　　　國香慢　書元忠

一幢湘魂正捐瑞水潤訊琴煙昏
江皋幾叢恨悴尚伴靈均日莫
通詞何許有嬋媛北渚孤嬋
國香繼流落未許東風換去荻
根　經年已國恨料鋼瞉冷
透鉛淚潛痕坟宮天遠鶯管
從此無春補他宣酥殘謹儀淌
凝老去王孫不成被花惱步入鷗
波滿襪秋塵　宣和畫譜無水仙
圖卷　嬾卿朱祖謀
　岑兒直題趙子固凌波

畫史會要․․․․․․․․․․․

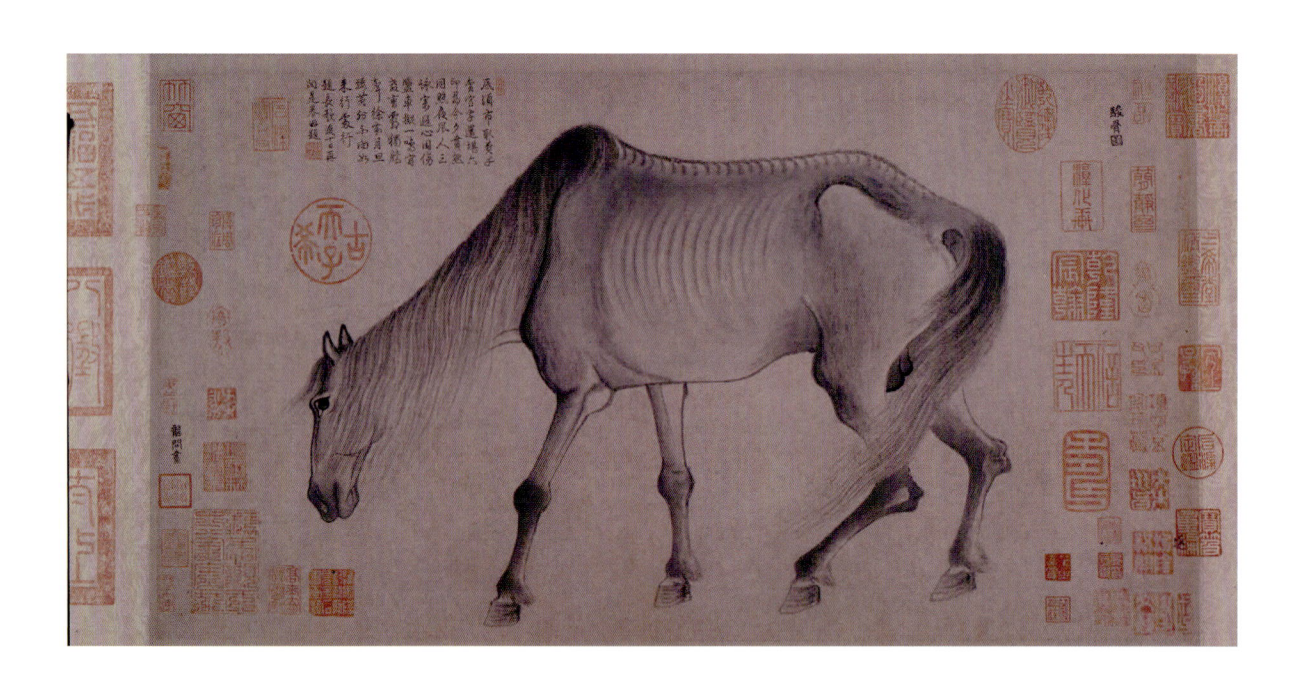

112. 骏骨图

宋或元
龚开
纸本水墨
手卷
纵29.9、横56.9厘米
大阪市立美术馆

Emaciated Horse

Song dynasty (960–1279) or Yuan dynasty (1271–1368)
Gong Kai
Ink on paper
Handscroll
H×W : 29.9×56.9 cm
The Osaka City Museum of Fine Arts

113. 墨兰图

南宋
郑思肖
纸本水墨
手卷
纵25.7、横42.4厘米
大阪市立美术馆

Ink Orchid

Southern Song dynasty (1127–1279)
Zheng Sixiao
Ink on paper
Handscroll
H×W : 25.7×42.4 cm
The Osaka City Museum of Fine Arts

送郝玄明使秦

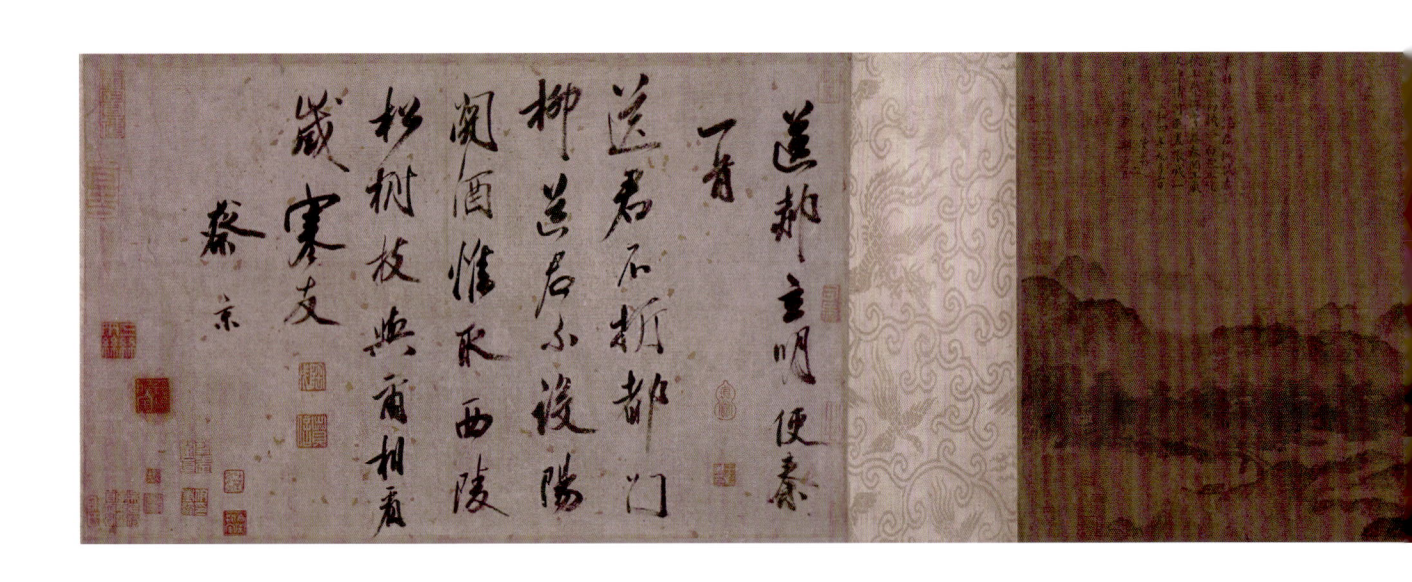

送君不折新都门
柳送君不后阳
关酒惟取西陵
杉树枝与甫相看
岁寒支

蔡京

114. 送郝玄明使秦图

南宋
胡舜臣
绢本设色
手卷
纵29.5、横111.5厘米
大阪市立美术馆

Farewell to Hao Xuanming Envoy

Southern Song dynasty (1127–1279)
Hu Shunchen
Ink and color on silk
Handscroll
H×W: 29.5×111.5 cm
The Osaka City Museum of Fine Arts

115. 罗汉浣衣图

南宋淳熙五年（公元1178年）
林庭珪
绢本设色
立轴
纵112.3、横53.5厘米
弗利尔美术馆

Luohan Laudering

Southern Song dynasty (1127–1279), dated 1178
Lin Tinggui
Ink and color on silk
Hanging scroll
H×W : 112.3×53.5 cm
The Freer Gallery of Art
Gift of Charles Lang Freer

116. 天台石桥图

南宋淳熙五年（公元1178年）
周季常
绢本设色
立轴
纵109.9、横52.7厘米
弗利尔美术馆

Rock Bridge at Mount Tiantai

Southern Song dynasty (1127–1279), dated 1178
Zhou Jichang
Ink and color on silk
Hanging scroll
H×W : 109.9×52.7 cm
The Freer Gallery of Art
Gift of Charles Lang Freer

117. 十王图之一

南宋
金处士
绢本设色
立轴
纵129.5、横49.5厘米
大都会艺术博物馆

Ten Kings of Hell

Southern Song dynasty (1127–1279)
Jin Chushi
Ink and color on silk
Hanging scroll
H×W : 129.5×49.5 cm
The Metropolitan Museum of Art
Rogers Fund, 1930

118. 十王图之二

南宋
金处士
绢本设色
立轴
纵129.5、横49.5厘米
大都会艺术博物馆

Ten Kings of Hell

Southern Song dynasty (1127–1279)
Jin Chushi
Ink and color on silk
Hanging scroll
H×W : 129.5×49.5 cm
The Metropolitan Museum of Art
Rogers Fund, 1930

119. 十王图之三

南宋
金处士
绢本设色
立轴
纵129.5、横49.5厘米
大都会艺术博物馆

Ten Kings of Hell

Southern Song dynasty (1127–1279)
Jin Chushi
Ink and color on silk
Hanging scroll
H×W : 129.5×49.5 cm
The Metropolitan Museum of Art
Rogers Fund, 1930

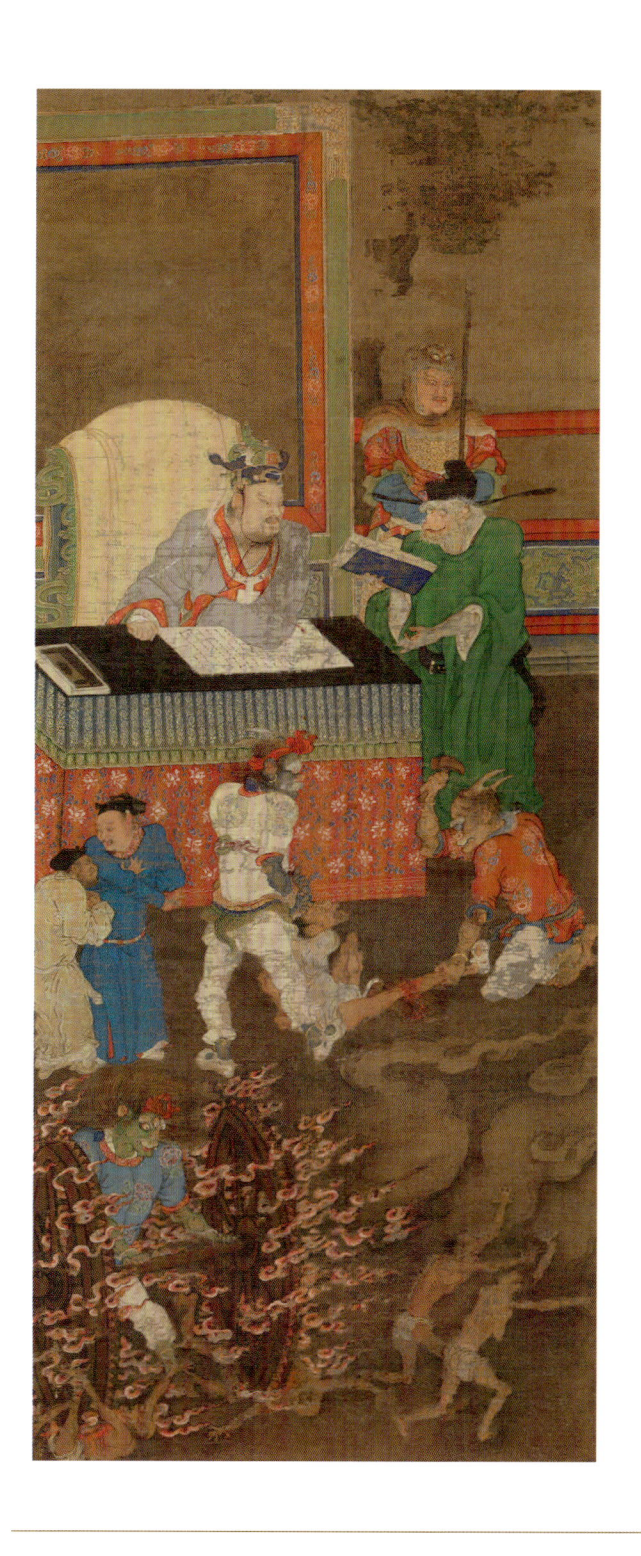

120. 十王图之四

南宋
金处士
绢本设色
立轴
纵129.5、横49.5厘米
大都会艺术博物馆

Ten Kings of Hell

Southern Song dynasty (1127–1279)
Jin Chushi
Ink and color on silk
Hanging scroll
H×W : 129.5×49.5 cm
The Metropolitan Museum of Art
Rogers Fund, 1930

121. 十王图之五

南宋
金处士
绢本设色
立轴
纵129.5、横49.5厘米
大都会艺术博物馆

Ten Kings of Hell

Southern Song dynasty (1127–1279)
Jin Chushi
Ink and color on silk
Hanging scroll
H×W : 129.5×49.5 cm
The Metropolitan Museum of Art
Rogers Fund, 1930

122. 十六罗汉图

南宋

金大受

绢本设色

立轴

每联：纵118.8、横51.7厘米

东京国立博物馆

Sixteen Arhats

Southern Song dynasty (1127–1279)

Jin Dashou

Ink and color on silk

Hanging scroll

H×W（each scroll）:118.8×51.7 cm

The Tokyo National Museum

ColBase(https://colbase.nich.go.jp/collection_items/tnm/TA-298?locale=ja)

058

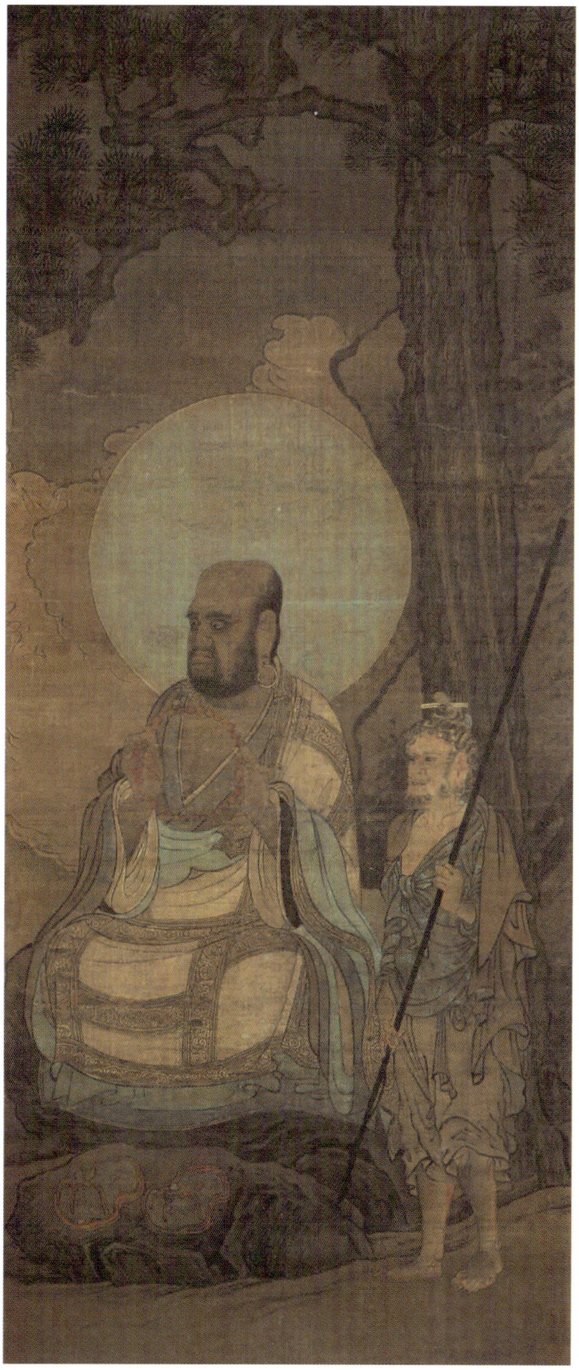

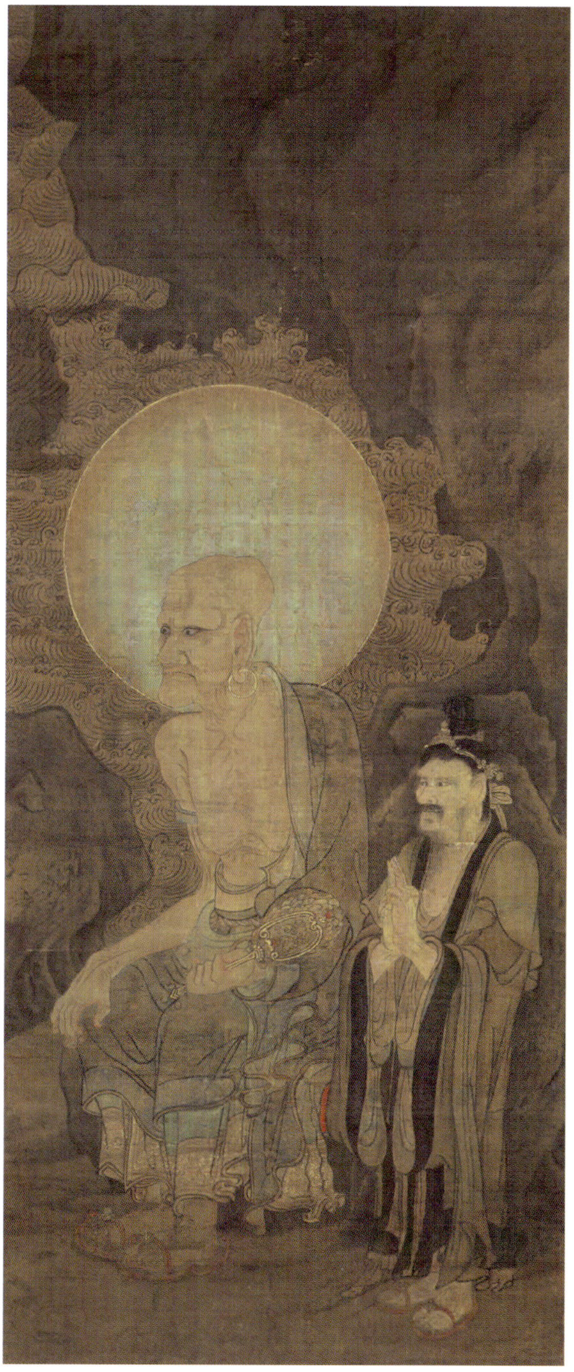

060

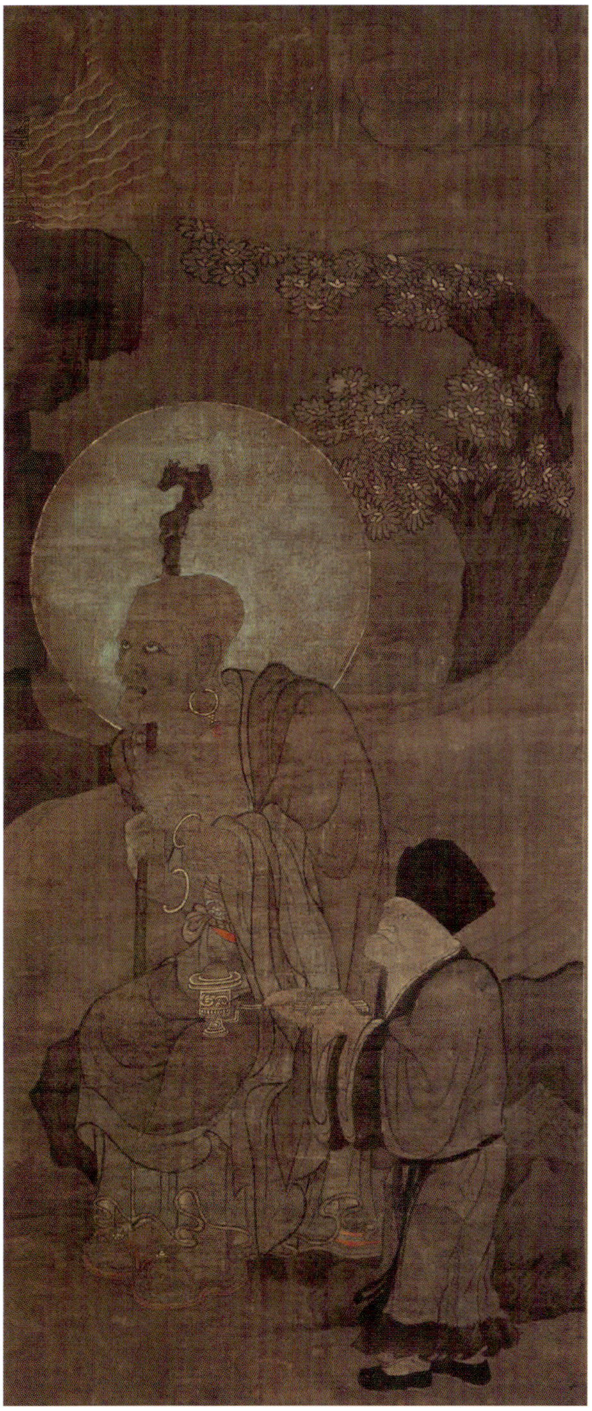

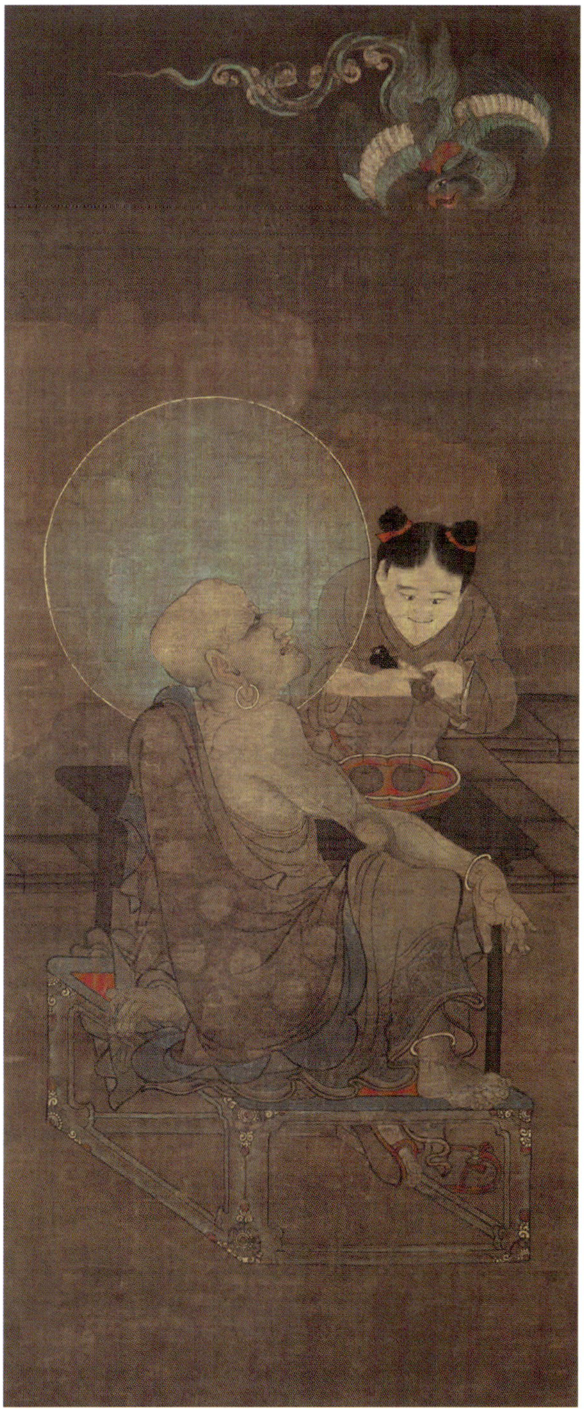

123. 妙法莲华经之观世音菩萨像   Avalokitesvara Bodhisattva

北宋	Northern Song dynasty (960–1127)
佚名	Artist unknown
绢本设色	Ink and color on silk
立轴	Hanging scrolls
纵84.1、横61.2厘米	H×W : 84.1×61.2 cm
集美博物馆	The Guimet Museum
	© RMN-Grand Palais (MNAAG, Paris) / image musée Guimet

124. 释迦出山图

南宋
佚名
纸本水墨
立轴
纵166.4、横49.9厘米
克利夫兰美术馆

Sakyamuni Emerging from Mountains

Southern Song dynasty (1127–1279)
Artist unknown
Ink on paper
Hanging scroll
H×W : 166.4×49.9 cm
The Cleveland Museum of Art
John L. Severance Fund 1970.2

125. 阿弥陀佛像

南宋
佚名
绢本设色
立轴
纵104.5、横53.7厘米
大都会艺术博物馆

Buddha Amitabha Descending from His Pure Land

Southern Song dynasty (1127–1279)
Artist unknown
Ink and color on silk
Hanging scroll
H×W : 104.5×53.7 cm
The Metropolitan Museum of Art
Rogers Fund, 1987

126. 阿弥陀佛像

南宋
佚名
绢本设色
立轴
纵135.9、横58.4厘米
大都会艺术博物馆

Buddha Amitabha Descending from his Pure Land

Southern Song dynasty (1127–1279)
Artist unknown
Ink and color on silk
Hanging scrolls
H×W : 135.9×58.4 cm
The Metropolitan Museum of Art
Purchase, The Dillon Fund Gift, 1980

127. 阿弥陀佛图

南宋
佚名
绢本设色
立轴
纵97.1、横53.8厘米
波士顿艺术博物馆

Amitabha Trinity Descending on Clouds

Southern Song dynasty (1127–1279)
Artist unknown
Ink and color on silk
Hanging scroll
H×W : 97.1×53.8 cm
The Museum of Fine Arts, Boston
Denman Waldo Ross Collection
© 2024 Museum of Fine Arts, Boston

128. 观音像

南宋
佚名
绢本设色
立轴
纵89.5、横41厘米
波士顿艺术博物馆

Bodhisattva Avalokitesvara and Immortal Shancai Crossing Sea

Southern Song dynasty (1127–1279)
Artist unknown
Ink and color on silk
Hanging scroll
H×W : 89.5×41 cm
The Museum of Fine Arts, Boston
William Sturgis Bigelow Collection
© 2024 Museum of Fine Arts, Boston

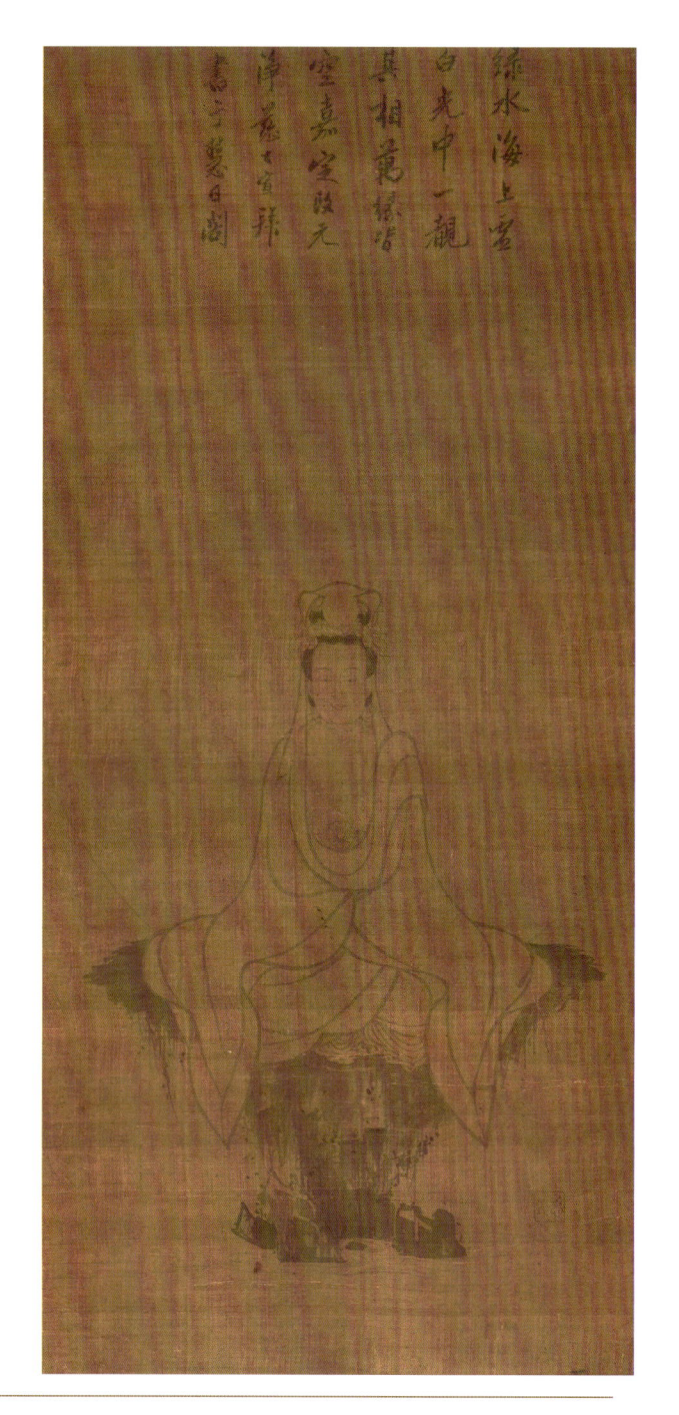

129. 白衣观音坐像

White-robed Budhisattva Avalokitesvara on Rock

南宋
佚名
绢本水墨
立轴
纵77.5、横37厘米
普林斯顿大学美术馆

Southern Song dynasty (1127–1279)
Artist unknown
Ink on silk
Hanging scroll
H×W : 77.5×37 cm
The Princeton University Art Museum
Bequest of John B. Elliott, Class of 1951
© 2024. Princeton University Art Museum/Art Resource NY/Scala, Florence

130. 普贤菩萨像

南宋
佚名
绢本设色
立轴
纵114.8、横55.1厘米
克利夫兰美术馆

Samantabhadra

Southern Song dynasty (1127–1279)
Artist unknown
Ink and color on silk
Hanging scroll
H×W : 114.8×55.1 cm
The Cleveland Museum of Art
Mr. and Mrs. William H. Marlatt Fund 1962.161

131. 文殊菩萨像

南宋
佚名
绢本设色
立轴
纵104、横54厘米
波士顿艺术博物馆

Manjusri on Lion with Attendant

Southern Song dynasty (1127–1279)
Artist unknown
Ink and color on silk
Hanging scroll
H×W : 104×54 cm
The Museum of Fine Arts, Boston
Museum purchase with funds donated by Mrs. Walter Scott Fitz
© 2024 Museum of Fine Arts, Boston

132. 阿弥陀佛与胁侍菩萨像

南宋
佚名
绢本设色
立轴
纵134、横79.7厘米
克利夫兰美术馆

Buddha Amitabha with Two Attending Bodhisattvas

Southern Song dynasty (1127–1279)
Artist unknown
Ink and color on silk
Hanging scroll
H×W : 134×79.7 cm
The Cleveland Museum of Art
Leonard C. Hanna, Jr. Fund 1974.35

133. 达摩面壁图

北宋
佚名
绢本水墨
立轴
纵203.2、横63.5厘米
克利夫兰美术馆

Bodhidharma Meditating Facing Cliff

Northern Song dynasty (960–1127)
Artist unknown
Ink on silk
Hanging scroll
H×W : 203.2×63.5 cm
The Cleveland Museum of Art
John L. Severance Fund 1972.41

134. 十六罗汉像

南宋
佚名
绢本设色
立轴
纵81.8、横37厘米
波士顿艺术博物馆

Sixteen Arhats

Southern Song dynasty (1127–1279)
Artist unknown
Ink and color on silk
Hanging scroll
H×W : 81.8×37 cm
The Museum of Fine Arts, Boston
William Sturgis Bigelow Collection
© 2024 Museum of Fine Arts, Boston

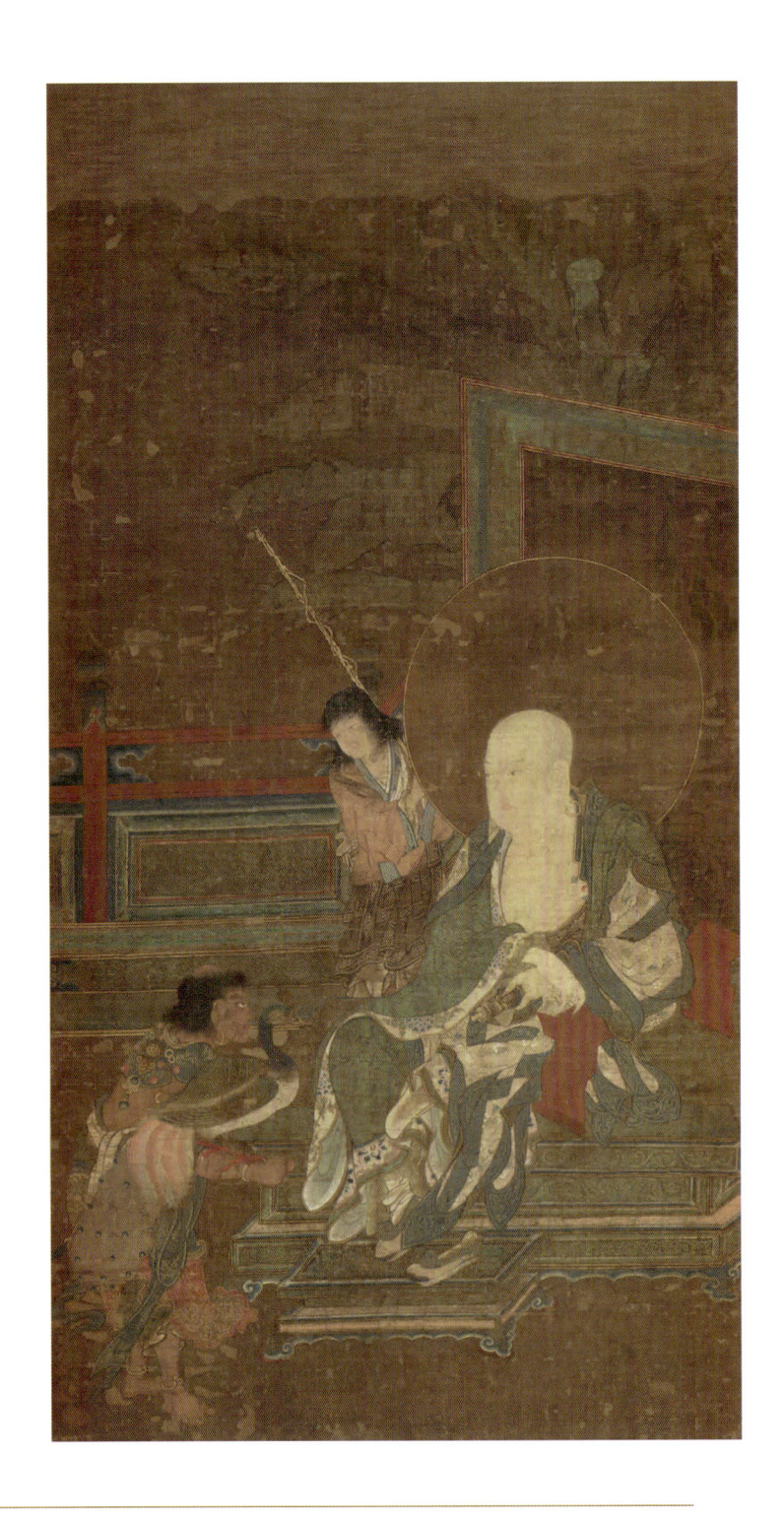

135. 罗汉坐像

南宋
佚名
绢本设色
立轴
纵201、横75.5厘米
克利夫兰美术馆

Seated Arhat with Two Attendants

Southern Song dynasty (1127–1279)
Artist unknown
Ink and color on silk
Hanging scroll
H×W : 201×75.5 cm
The Cleveland Museum of Art
John L. Severance Fund 1976.91

136. 静坐罗汉像

宋或元
佚名
绢本设色
立轴
纵115.5、横52.1厘米
耶鲁大学艺术博物馆

Fifth Luohan Nakula

Song dynasty (960–1279) or Yuan dynasty (1271–1368)
Artist unknown
Ink and color on silk
Hanging scroll
H×W : 115.5×52.1 cm
The Yale University Art Gallery
Gift of Mrs. Jared K. Morse

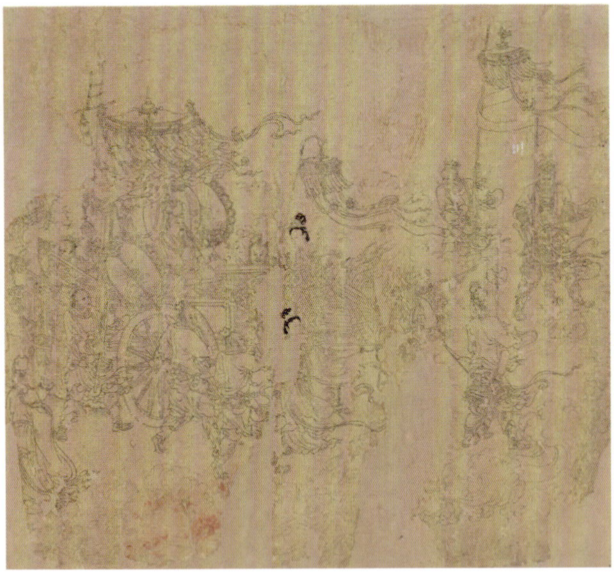

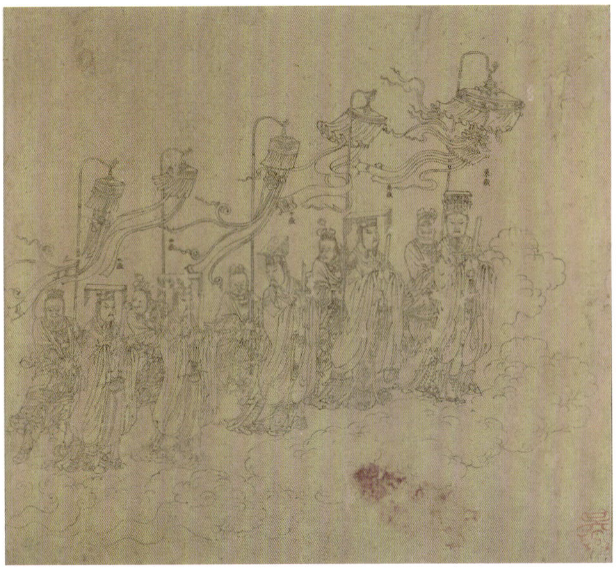

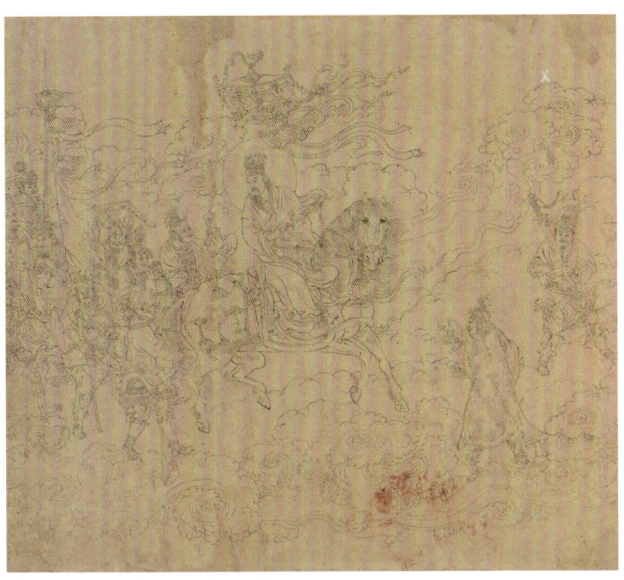

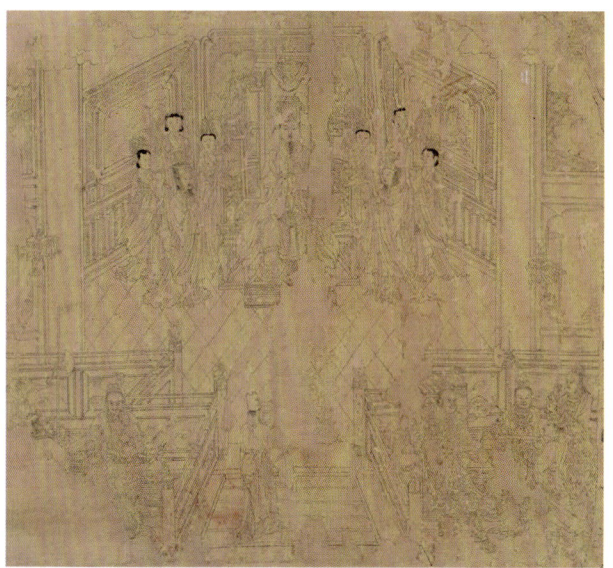

137. 佛道主题画册（选十）   Album of Daoist and Buddhist Themes

南宋
（传）吴道子
纸本水墨
册页
每开：纵34.3、横38.6厘米
克利夫兰美术馆

Southern Song dynasty (1127–1279)
Attributed to Wu Daozi
Ink on paper
Album leaf
H×W(each leaf) : 34.3×38.6 cm
The Cleveland Museum of Art
John L. Severance Fund in honor of Dr. Ju-hsi Chou and Gift of various donors to the department of Asian Art (by exchange) 2004.1

078

138. 洞天论道图

南宋
佚名
绢本设色
册页
纵24.8、横25.2厘米
大都会艺术博物馆

Conversation in Cave

Southern Song dynasty (1127–1279)
Artist unknown
Ink and color on silk
Album leaf
H×W : 24.8×25.2 cm
The Metropolitan Museum of Art
From the Collection of A. W. Bahr, Purchase, Fletcher Fund, 1947

道光辛丑十月
桐城姚元之書

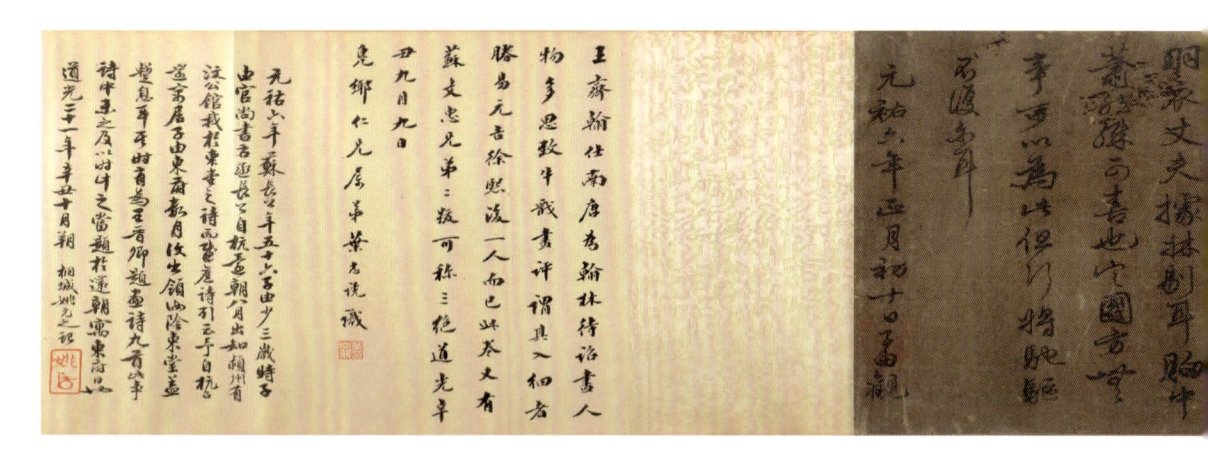

朅家丈夫擄林劇耳貽中
蕭頔孫而書也宅國吉崦
辛垂以為此偘们將馳馳
武邇東耳
元祐六年正月初十四日画觀

王齋翰住南唐為翰林待詔畫人
物多思致半戲畫評謂其入神者
勝為元吉徐熙後一人而已此卷丈有
蘇支忠兄第三版可稱三絕道光辛
丑九月九日
亮卿仁兄居弟葉名琛識

元祐六年蘇長公年五十六公由少三歲時子
由官尚書右丞長公自杭壽朝八月出知穎州有
汝公館栽柜東齋之詩而聲虛朝詩引云予自杭
還寓居子由東齋歆月汝出餉幽陰東齋益
豐鬼耳年時有為王晉卿題畫詩九首內半
詩中朱之庼対中之當題於適朝寓東齋凰
道光三十一年辛丑十月朔 桐城姚元之記

南唐王詩挑耳

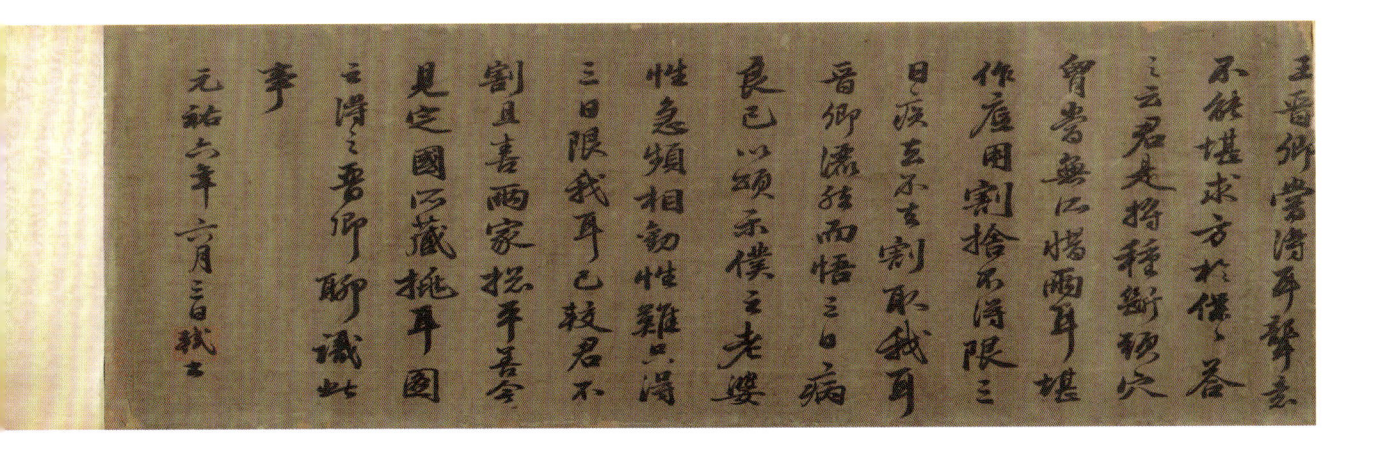

王晉卿嘗遺予聲畫
不旋踵求方於僕~答
之云君无以燭雨耳塞
曾當用燭捨不得限三
日疲玄不言割取戕耳
晉卿流狂而悟三日病
良已以頌示僕云老婆
性急頻相勸性難改得
三日限我耳己較君不
割且喜兩家撚平喜舍
見之國所藏挑耳圖
云浔之晉卿聊識此
事
元祐六年六月三日軾書

139. 挑耳图

北宋
佚名
绢本设色
手卷
纵25.1、横47.6厘米
大都会艺术博物馆

Library Scene

Northern Song dynasty (960–1127)
Artist unknown
Ink and color on silk
Handscroll
H×W: 25.1×47.6 cm
The Metropolitan Museum of Art
From the Collection of A. W. Bahr,
Purchase, Fletcher Fund, 1947

082

140. 吕洞宾过岳阳楼图

宋或元
佚名
绢本设色
册页
纵23.8、横25.1厘米
大都会艺术博物馆

Immortal Lv Dongbin Appearing over Yueyang Pavilion

Song dynasty (960–1279) or Yuan dynasty (1271–1368)
Artist unknown
Ink and color on silk
Album leaf
H×W : 23.8×25.1 cm
The Metropolitan Museum of Art
Rogers Fund, 1917

141. 射雁图

南宋
佚名
绢本设色
册页
纵21、横23.4厘米
克利夫兰美术馆

Three Horsemen Hunting Wild Geese

Southern Song dynasty (1127–1279)
Artist unknown
Ink and color on silk
Album leaf
H×W : 21×23.4 cm
The Cleveland Museum of Art
Gift of the John Huntington Art and
Polytechnic Trust 1915.703

142. 樵夫归家图

南宋
佚名
绢本水墨
立轴
纵124.5、横58.3厘米
克利夫兰美术馆

Woodcutters Returning Home

Southern Song dynasty (1127–1279)
Artist unknown
Ink on silk
Hanging scroll
H×W : 124.5×58.3 cm
The Cleveland Museum of Art
Leonard C. Hanna, Jr. Fund 1988.20

143. 狸奴婴戏图

南宋
佚名
绢本设色
团扇
纵24.5、横25.7厘米
波士顿艺术博物馆

Child with his Pets in Flower Garden

Southern Song dynasty (1127–1279)
Artist unknown
Ink and color on silk
Round fan
H×W : 24.5×25.7 cm
The Museum of Fine Arts, Boston
Chinese and Japanese Special Fund
© 2024 Museum of Fine Arts, Boston

144. 牧牛图

南宋
佚名
绢本设色
册页
纵24.7、横25.6厘米
大阪市立美术馆

Cowherd from Album of Old Master Paintings

Southern Song dynasty (1127–1279)
Artist unknown
Ink and color on silk
Album leaf
H×W : 24.7×25.6 cm
The Osaka City Museum of Fine Arts

145. 牧牛图

南宋
佚名
绢本水墨
册页
纵24.1、横25.2厘米
波士顿艺术博物馆

Herd-boy Mounting Water Buffalo

Southern Song dynasty (1127–1279)
Artist unknown
Ink on silk
Album leaf
H×W : 24.1×25.2 cm
The Museum of Fine Arts, Boston
Denman Waldo Ross Collection
© 2024 Museum of Fine Arts, Boston

146. 骑驴图

南宋
佚名
纸本水墨
立轴
纵64.1、横33厘米
大都会艺术博物馆

Chan Master Riding Mule

Southern Song dynasty (1127–1279)
Artist unknown
Ink on paper
Hanging scroll
H×W : 64.1×33 cm
The Metropolitan Museum of Art
Bequest of John M. Crawford Jr., 1988

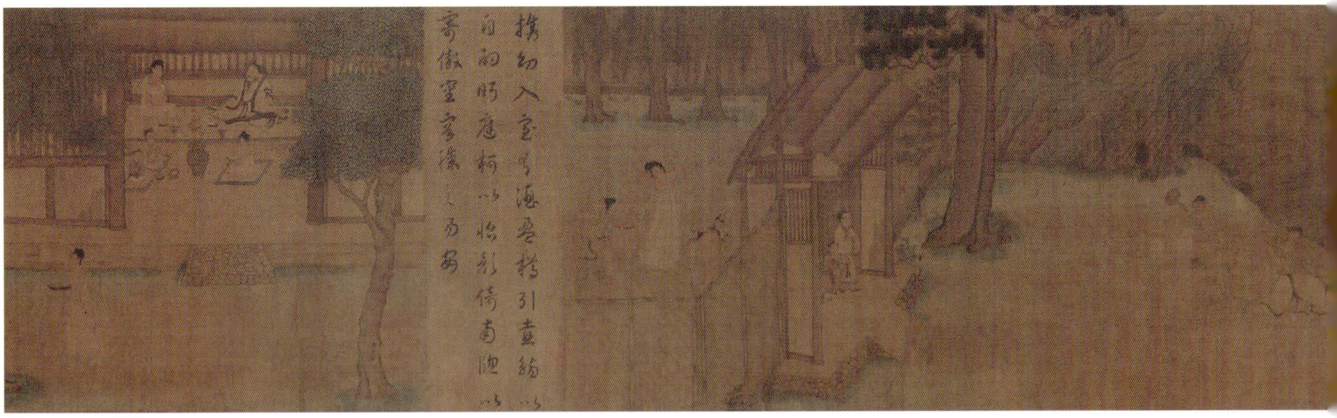

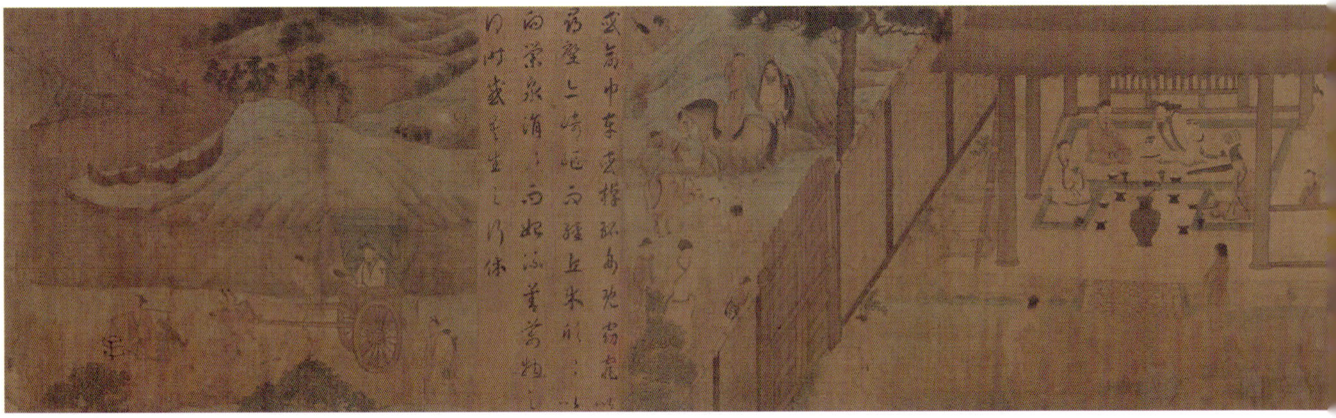

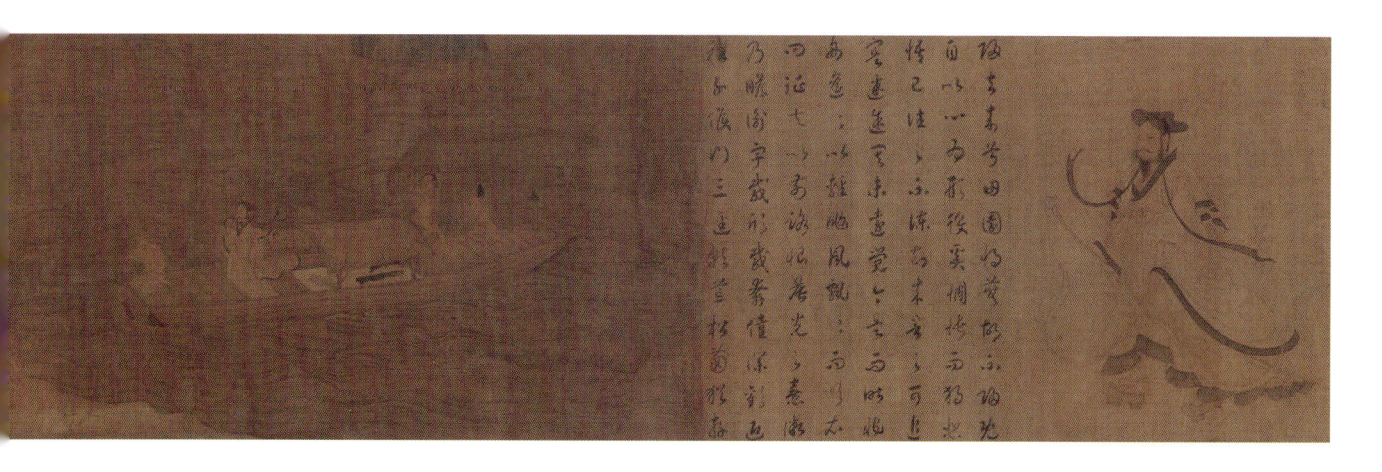

147. 归去来兮辞图

南宋
佚名
绢本设色
手卷
纵30、横438.6厘米
波士顿美术博物馆

Illustrations to Tao Qian's Prose Poem "Homecoming"

Southern Song dynasty (1127–1279)
Artist unknown
Ink and color on silk
Handscroll
H×W: 30×438.6 cm
The Museum of Fine Arts, Boston
Chinese and Japanese Special Fund
20.757
© 2024 Museum of Fine Arts, Boston

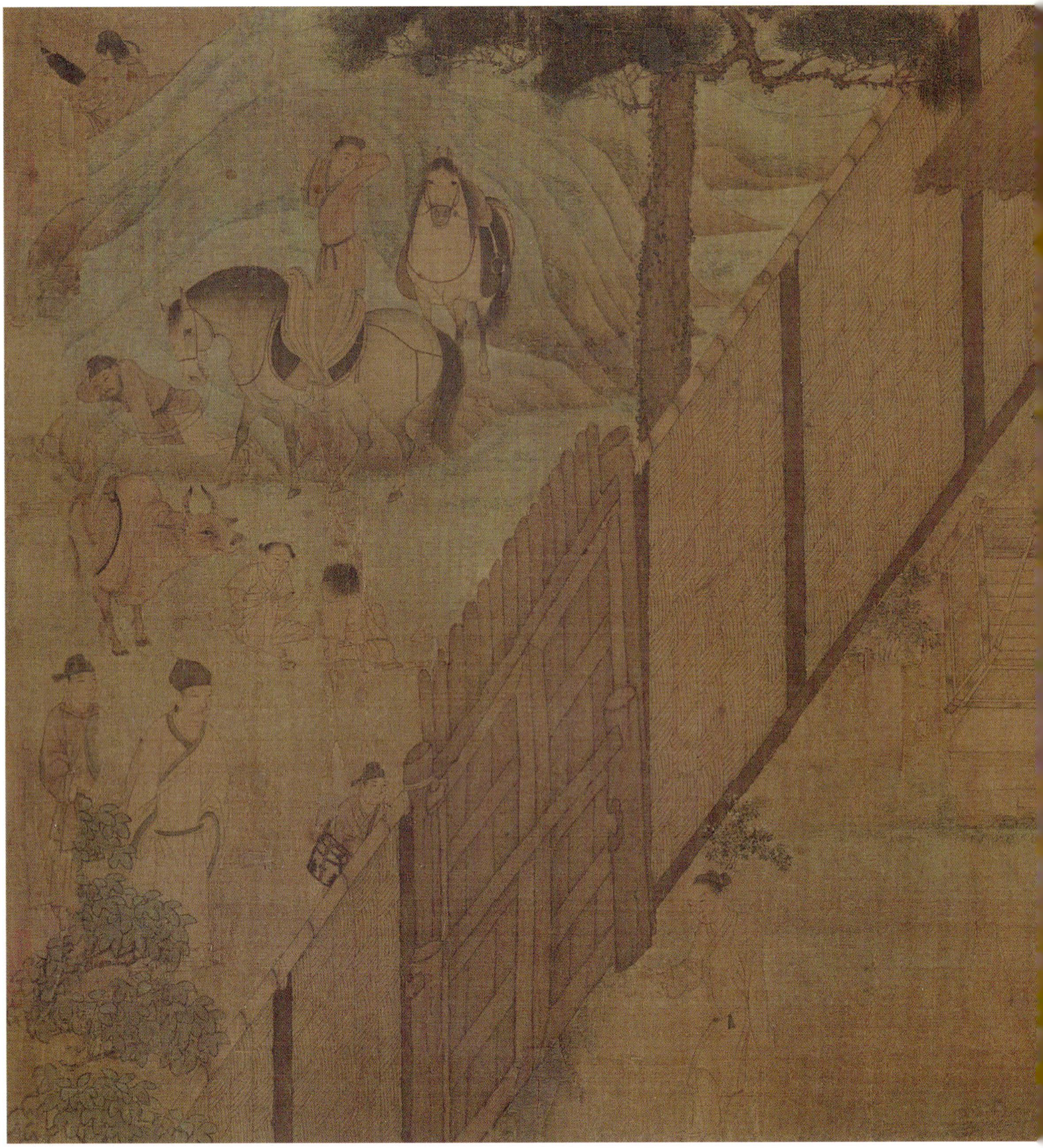

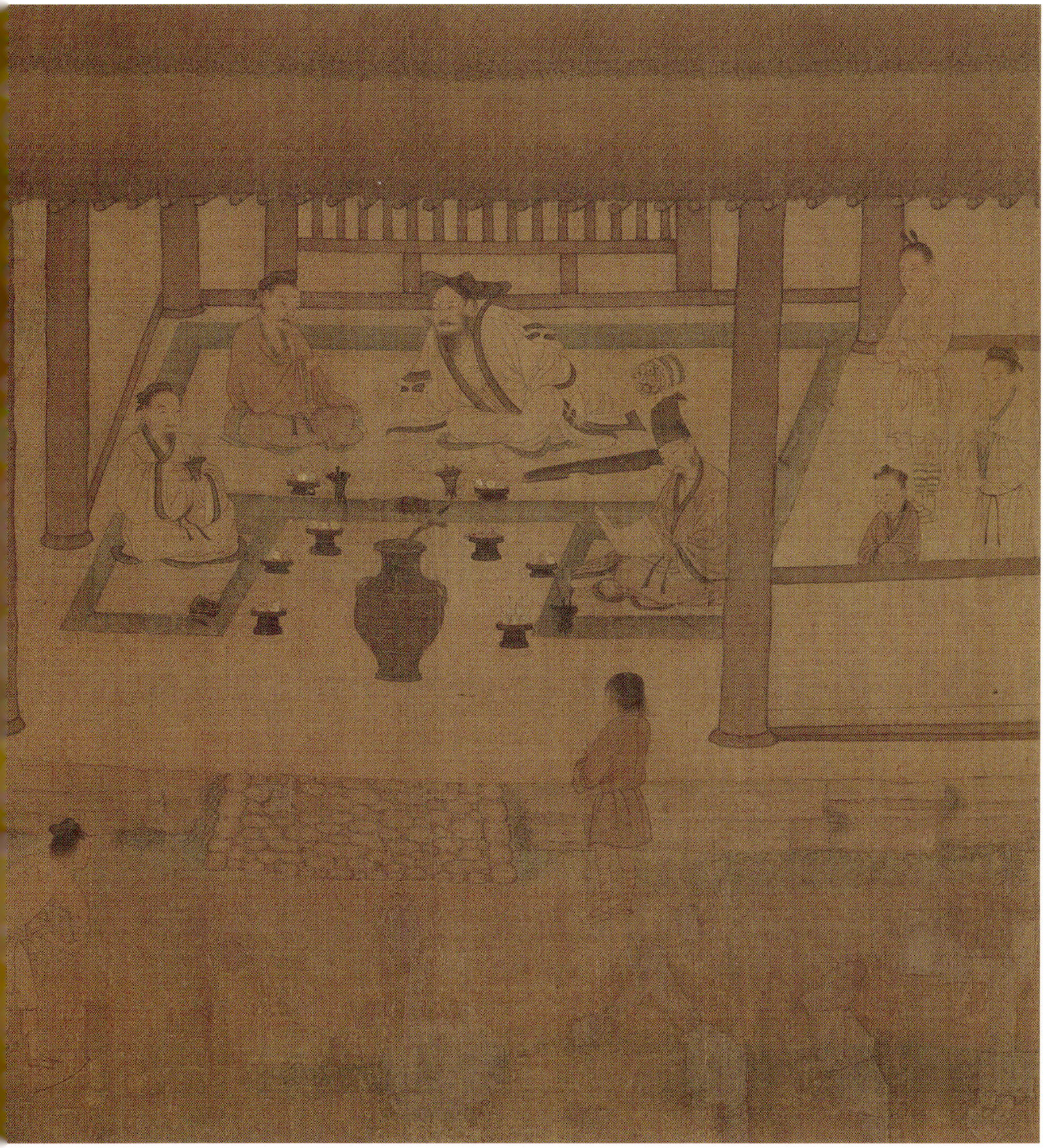

148. 庞灵照图

南宋
佚名
绢本设色
册页
纵24.5、横25.6厘米
波士顿美术博物馆

Snowscape with Standing Woman

Southern Song dynasty (1127–1279)
Artist unknown
Ink and color on silk
Album leaf
H×W : 24.5×25.6 cm
The Museum of Fine Arts, Boston
Chinese and Japanese Special Fund 05.204
© 2024 Museum of Fine Arts, Boston

149. 草堂对坐图

南宋
佚名
绢本设色
册页
纵26、横27.3厘米
克利夫兰美术馆

Conversation in Thatched Hut

Southern Song dynasty (1127–1279)
Artist unknown
Ink and color on silk
Album leaf
H×W : 26×27.3 cm
The Cleveland Museum of Art
Mr. and Mrs. William H. Marlatt Fund 1975.21

鎮海軍浙江東西荊南等道節度使中書令晉國公韓滉畫
按唐書韓公天縱聰明神翰正直出入顯重周旋令猷在
德宗朝值兹喪亂遂熏統六道即制法律嚴肅萬里無虞然常
愛丹青調格高逸在僧繇子虔之上能圖田家風俗及人物
特畫精妙品居上上

150. 田家风俗图

宋或元
佚名
绢本设色
手卷
纵25.1、横91.1厘米
耶鲁大学艺术博物馆

Peasants Moving

Song dynasty (960–1279) or Yuan dynasty (1271–1368)
Artist unknown
Ink and color on silk
Handscroll
H×W : 25.1×91.1 cm
The Yale University Art Gallery
Gift of Earl Morse

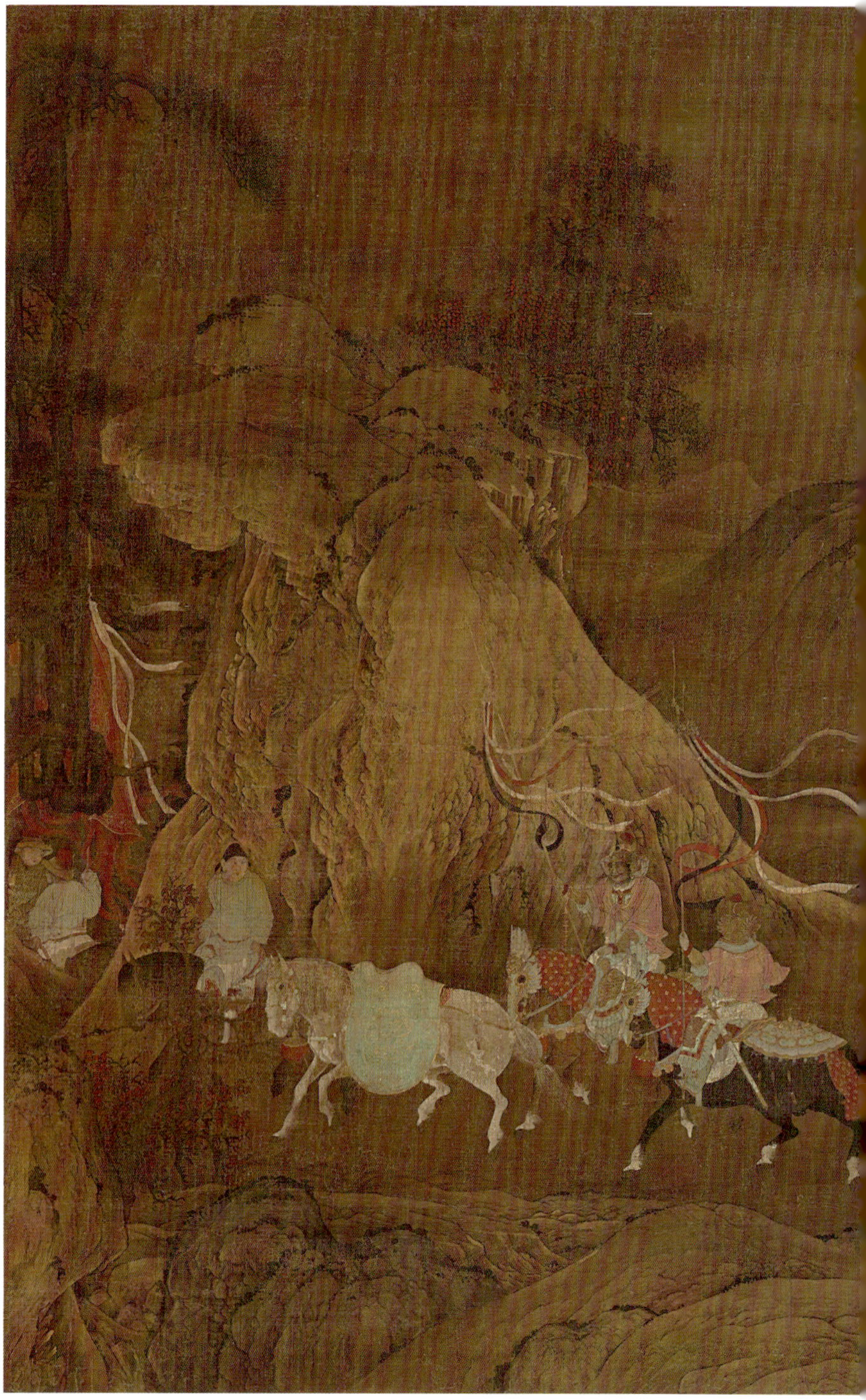

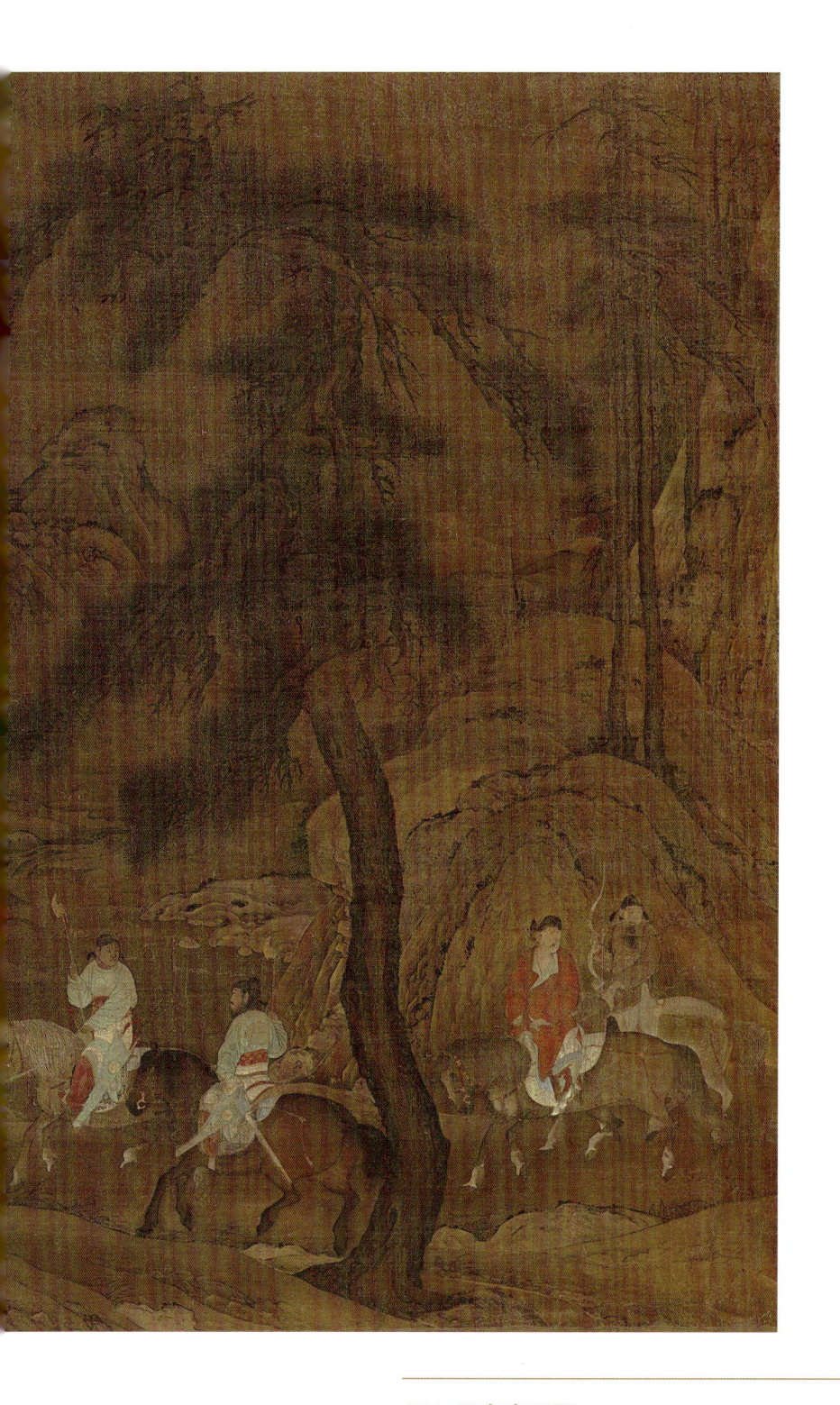

151. 明皇幸蜀图

南宋
佚名
绢本设色
立轴
纵113.7、横82.9厘米
大都会艺术博物馆

Emperor Xuanzong's Flight to Shu

Southern Song dynasty (1127–1279)
Artist unknown
Ink and color on silk
Hanging scroll
H×W : 113.7×82.9 cm
The Metropolitan Museum of Art
Rogers Fund, 1941

152. 仙山楼阁图

宋
佚名
绢本设色
册页
纵33、横41.6厘米
克利夫兰美术馆

Palace Landscape

Song dynasty (960–1279)
Artist unknown
Ink and color on silk
Album leaf
H×W : 33×41.6 cm
The Cleveland Museum of Art
Purchase, The B. D. G. Leviton Foundation Gift,
in honor of Marie-Hélène and Guy Weill, 2003

153. 仿范宽山水图

北宋
佚名
绢本设色
立轴
纵166.1、横104.5厘米
大都会艺术博物馆

Landscape After Fan Kuan

Northern Song dynasty (960–1127)
Artist unknown
Ink and color on silk
Hanging scroll
H×W : 166.1×104.5 cm
The Metropolitan Museum of Art
Gift of Irene and Earl Morse, 1956

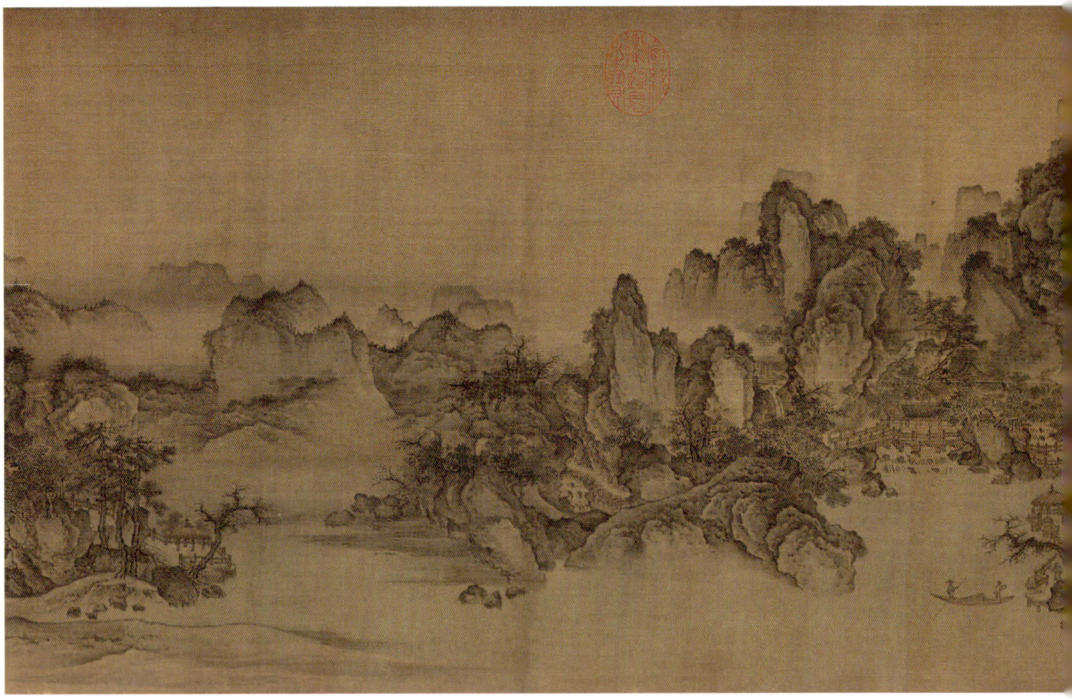

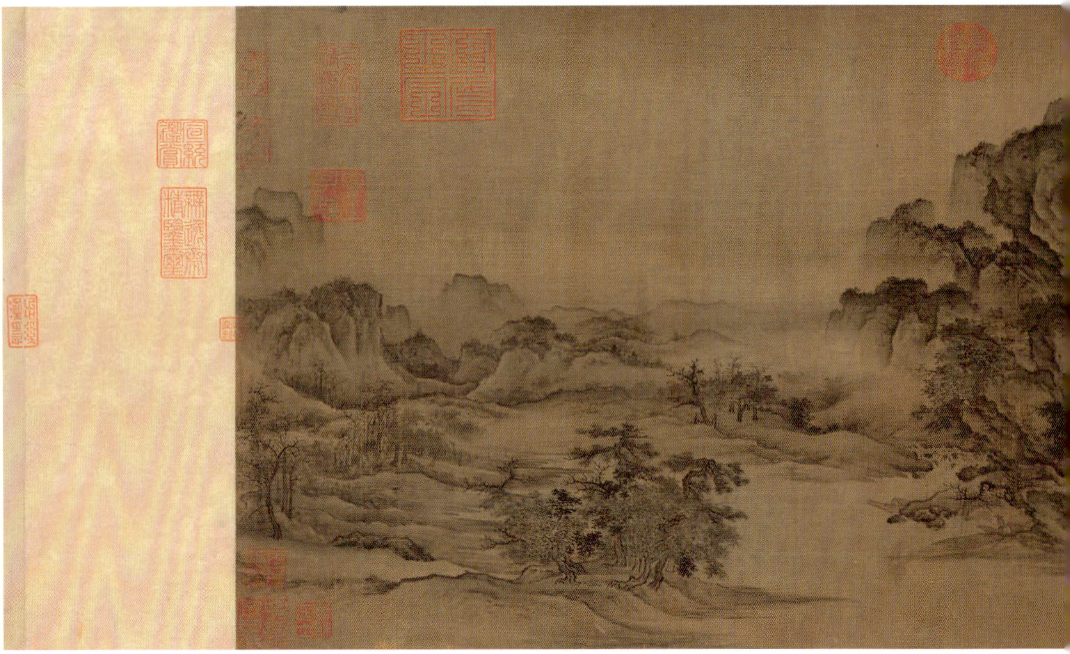

154. 溪山无尽图

金
佚名
绢本设色
手卷
纵35.1、横213厘米
克利夫兰美术馆

Streams and Mountains Without End

Jin dynasty (1115–1234)
Artist unknown
Ink and color on silk
Handscroll
H×W : 35.1×213 cm
The Cleveland Museum of Art
Purchase, The Dillon Fund Gift, 1976

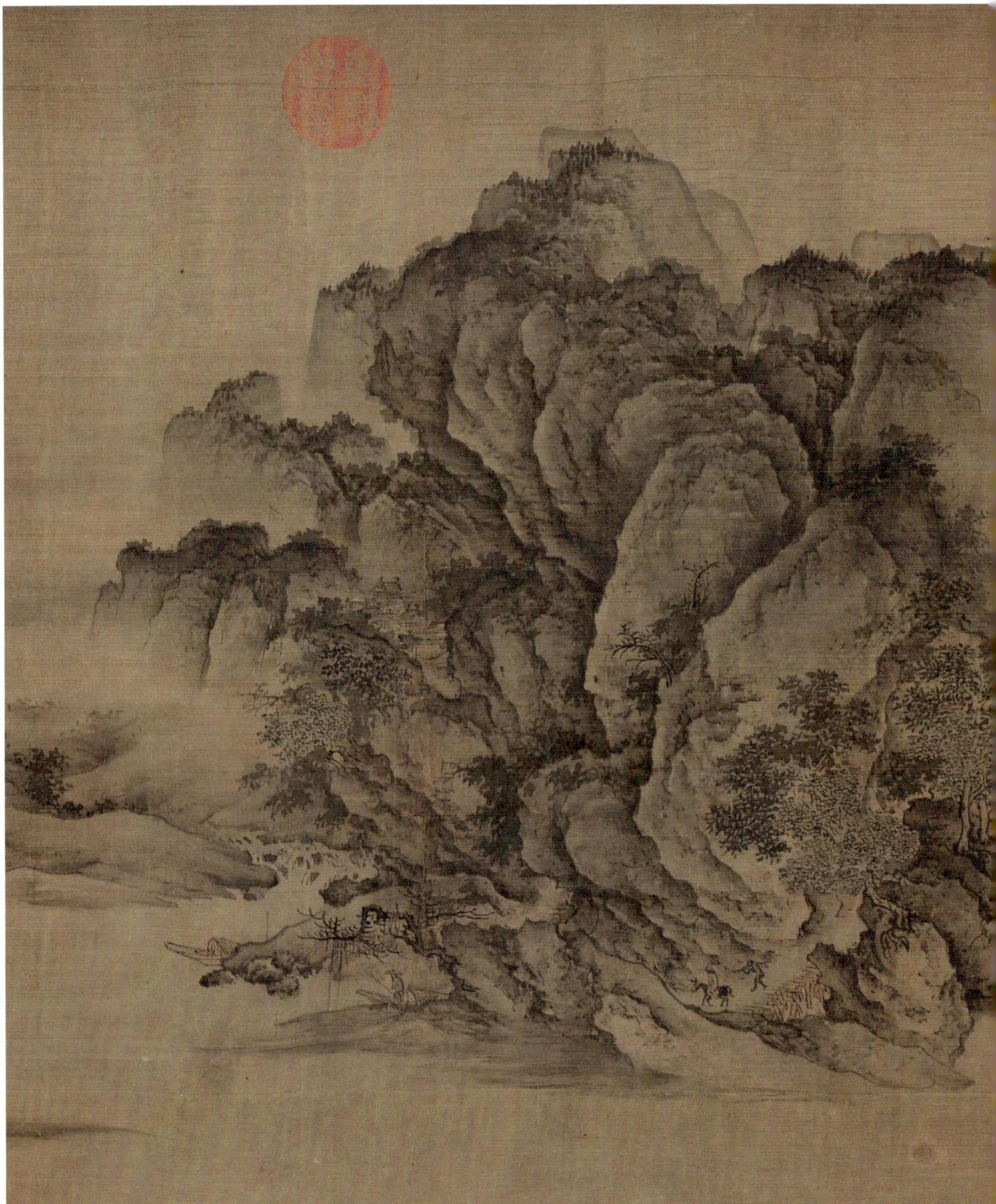

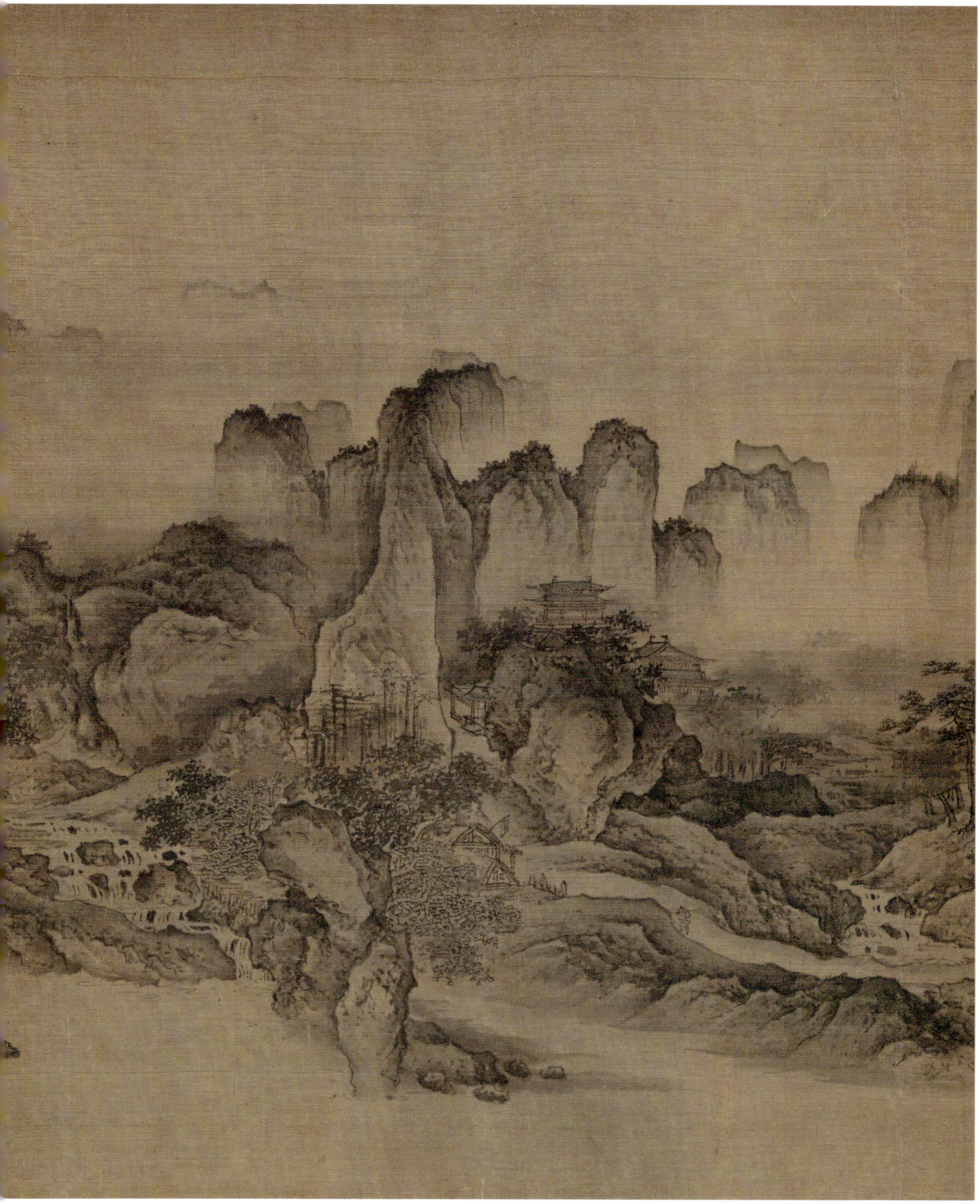

未央曾闢天家春碧闌瑤
砌無纖塵濃雲曉染宮樹
綠雙蛾暗為流鶯鞭長
楊有賦無人買畫裏猶
能見容來御溝流雨碧溶
香燕子歸未春已改

趙巖

徐青齋藏定徧伽藏拾金

155. 别苑春山图

南宋
佚名
绢本设色
手卷
纵26.2、横286.5厘米
大都会艺术博物馆

Retreats in Spring Hills

Southern Song dynasty (1127–1279)
Artist unknown
Ink and color on silk
Handscroll
H×W : 26.2×286.5 cm
The Metropolitan Museum of Art
Bequest of John M. Crawford Jr., 1988

156. 泛舟柳塘图

南宋
佚名
绢本设色
册页
纵23.3、横24.9厘米
大都会艺术博物馆

Boating by Willow Bank

Southern Song dynasty (1127–1279)
Artist unknown
Ink and color on silk
Album leaf
H×W：23.3×24.9 cm
The Metropolitan Museum of Art
From the Collection of A. W. Bahr, Purchase, Fletcher Fund, 1947

157. 江行图

南宋
佚名
绢本设色
团扇
纵25.3、横19.2厘米
克利夫兰美术馆

Boats at Anchor

Southern Song dynasty (1127–1279)
Artist unknown
Ink and color on silk
Round fan
H×W : 25.3×19.2 cm
The Cleveland Museum of Art
Bequest of Mrs. A. Dean Perry 1997.90

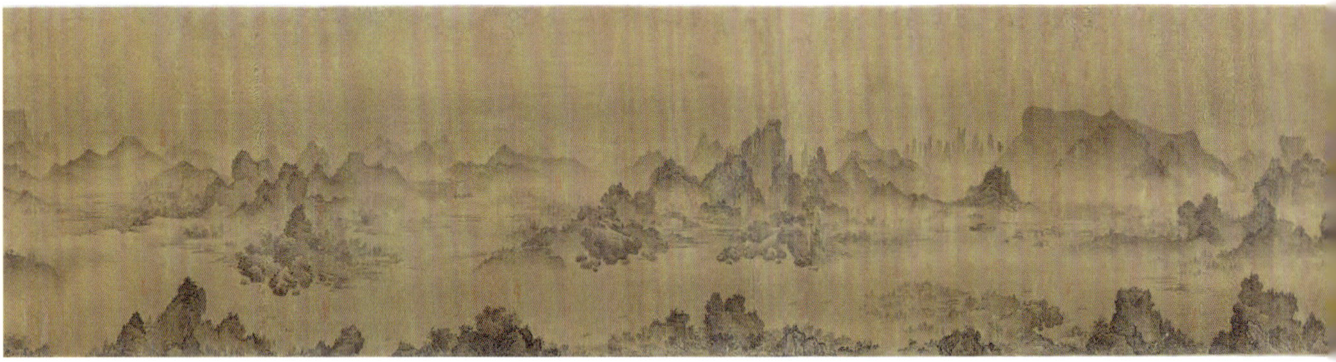

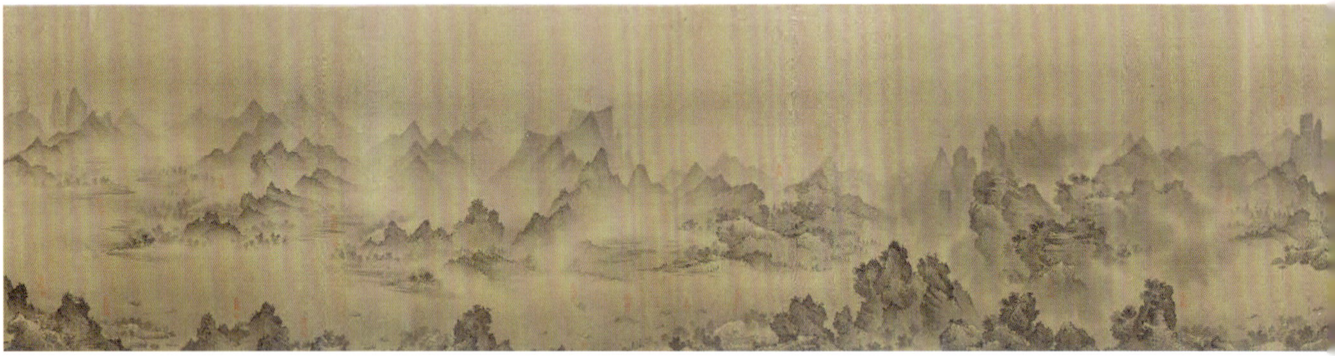

158. 长江万里图

宋或元
佚名
绢本水墨
手卷
纵43.5、横1656.6厘米
弗利尔美术馆

Ten Thousand Li Along Yangzi River

Song dynasty (960–1279) or Yuan dynasty (1271–1368)
Artist unknown
Ink on silk
Handscroll
H×W : 43.5×1656.6 cm
The Freer Gallery of Art
Gift of Charles Lang Freer

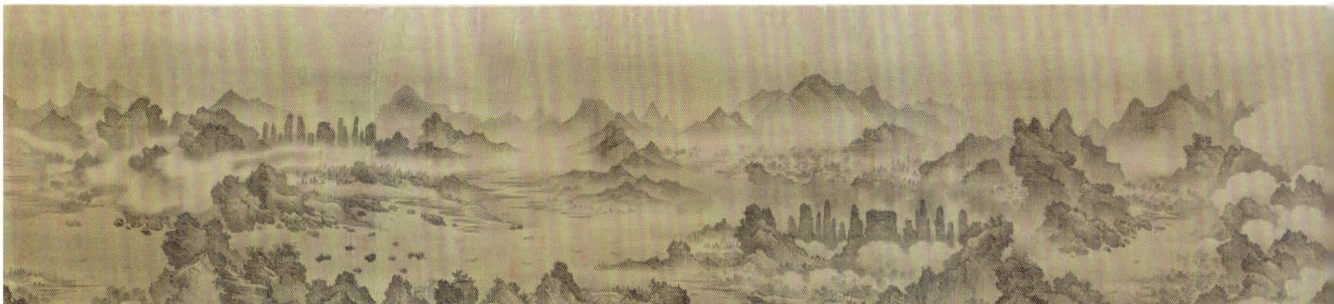

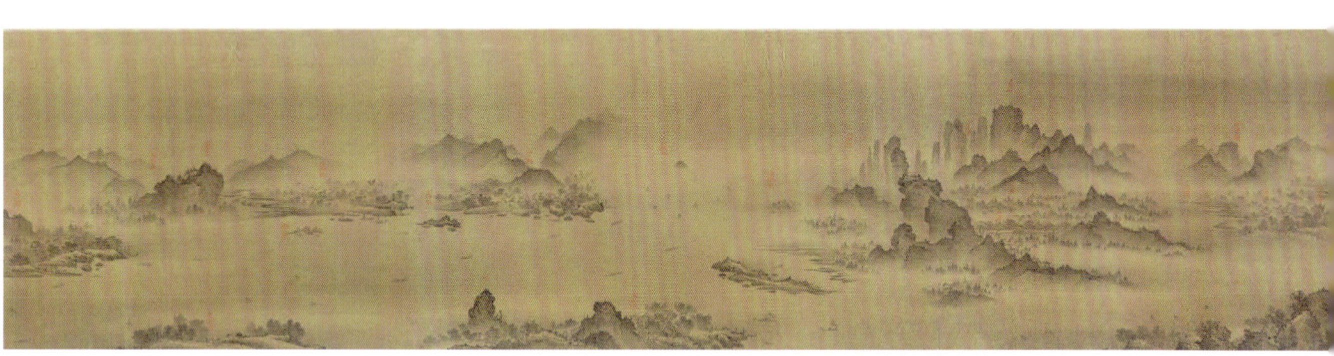

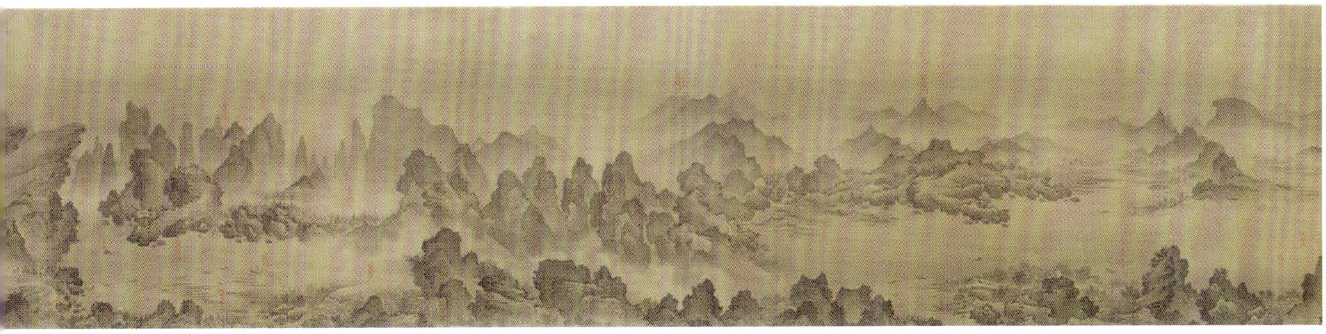

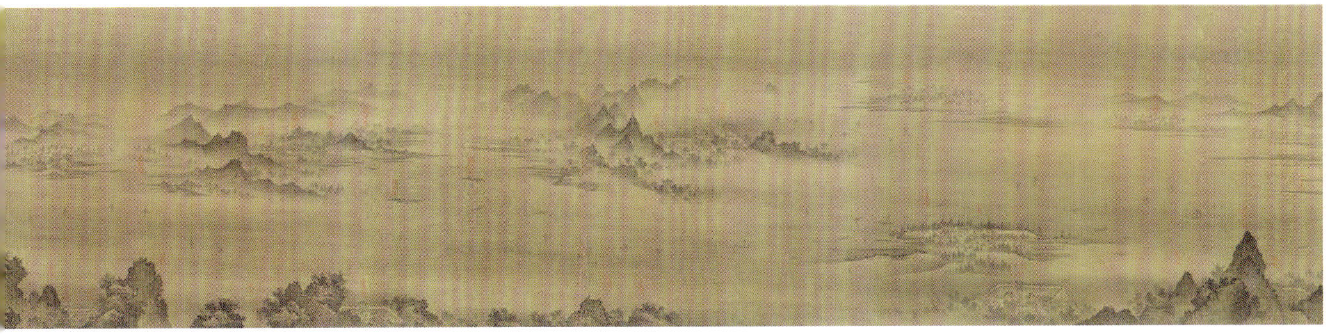

此卷長江萬里圖為今大条張夏山先生所藏予嘗於京口見米元暉澄心堂帝一卷筆勢奇恠有意外象家居時與人㩗至一卷夏圭墨氣古動可愛此卷則規模郭熙而平遠清潤肯不盡之趣宋董倚長江為湯池板者時畫手多喜為興之浩致夏山字用戴家金華之平不能筆而鐵騎飛渡矢刃相將所謂行住坐臥不離這箇耶復相占為之大笑是歲嘉靖甲午八月吉觀於江西郡司之紫薇樓下遂書雲間陸深子淵父

平嘗見李伯時表江西陳太僕家筆江携純五就此卷乃宣和御府所收當異在宣和宋以前名手蹟為夏家蹟繽用後与長心陸文裕跋砺左提戲賢五百藥奉之說孫㑳是也
已未中秋沈焞

115

159. 渡津图

南宋
佚名
绢本设色
册页
纵23.8、横25.2厘米
弗利尔美术馆

Waiting for Ferry

Southern Song dynasty (1127–1279)
Artist unknown
Ink and color on silk
Album leaf
H×W : 23.8×25.2 cm
The Freer Gallery of Art
Gift of Charles Lang Freer

160. 桃花春水图

南宋
佚名
绢本设色
册页
纵19.6、横21.5厘米
普林斯顿大学美术馆

Peach Blossoms by Spring River

Southern Song dynasty (1127–1279)
Artist unknown
Ink and color on silk
Album leaf
H×W : 19.6×21.5 cm
The Princeton University Art Museum
Gift of Mrs. Edward L. Elliott
© 2024. Princeton University Art Museum/Art Resource NY/Scala, Florence

161. 岸边柳树图

南宋
佚名
绢本设色
册页
纵23.8、横25.1厘米
克利夫兰美术馆

Willows

Southern Song dynasty (1127–1279)
Artist unknown
Ink and color on silk
Album leaf
H×W : 23.8×25.1 cm
The Cleveland Museum of Art
The Kelvin Smith Collection, given by Mrs. Kelvin Smith 1985.365

162. 雪桥送别图

北宋
佚名
绢本设色
册页
纵24.8、横26厘米
大都会艺术博物馆

Bridge in Snow

Northern Song dynasty (960–1127)
Artist unknown
Ink and color on silk
Album leaf
H×W : 24.8×26 cm
The Metropolitan Museum of Art
John Stewart Kennedy Fund, 1913

163. 归舟图

南宋
佚名
绢本设色
册页
纵24.4、横26厘米
大都会艺术博物馆

Towing Boat in Rainstorm

Southern Song dynasty (1127–1279)
Artist unknown
Ink and color on silk
Album leaf
H×W : 24.4×26 cm
The Metropolitan Museum of Art
From the Collection of A. W. Bahr, Purchase,
Fletcher Fund, 1947

164. 雪景图

宋或元	**Winter Scene**
佚名	Song dynasty (960–1279) or Yuan dynasty (1271–1368)
绢本水墨	Artist unknown
册页	Ink on silk
纵24、横24厘米	Album leaf
克利夫兰美术馆	H×W : 24×24 cm
	The Cleveland Museum of Art
	Gift of the John Huntington Art and Polytechnic Trust
	1915.699

165. 坐观云雾图

北宋	Northern Song dynasty (960–1127)
佚名	Artist unknown
绢本设色	Ink and color on silk
册页	Album leaf
纵23.7、横26.4厘米	H×W：23.7×26.4 cm
大都会艺术博物馆	The Metropolitan Museum of Art
	From the Collection of A. W. Bahr, Purchase, Fletcher Fund, 1947

Misty Landscape with Scholars and Attendants

166. 观瀑图

南宋
佚名
绢本设色
册页
纵22.8、横23厘米
大阪市立美术馆

Viewing Waterfall

Southern Song dynasty (1127–1279)
Artist unknown
Ink and color on silk
Album leaf
H×W : 22.8×23 cm
The Osaka City Museum of Fine Arts

167. 秋江渔艇图

宋或元
佚名
绢本设色
立轴
纵133.3、横56.2厘米
大阪市立美术馆

Fishing Boats on Autumn River

Song dynasty (960–1279) or Yuan dynasty (1271–1368)
Artist unknown
Ink and color on silk
Hanging scroll
H×W : 133.3×56.2 cm
The Osaka City Museum of Fine Arts

168. 渔舟图

南宋
佚名
绢本设色
册页
纵23.2、横23.8厘米
大都会艺术博物馆

Fishing Boat

Southern Song dynasty (1127–1279)
Artist unknown
Ink and color on silk
Album leaf
H×W : 23.2×23.8 cm
The Metropolitan Museum of Art
Bequest of Ellis Gray Seymour, 1948

馬遠山村策杖

169. 山村策杖图

宋或元
佚名
绢本设色
册页
纵22.5、横22.5厘米
耶鲁大学艺术博物馆

Retired Scholar Enjoying Mountain Scenery

Song dynasty (960–1279) or Yuan dynasty (1271–1368)
Artist unknown
Ink and color on silk
Album leaf
H×W : 22.5×22.5 cm
The Yale University Art Gallery
Gift of Dr. Howard Balensweig, B.S. 1943, and Mrs. Carolyn Balensweig

170. 雪山行旅图

南宋
佚名
绢本水墨
册页
纵24.3、横25.7厘米
弗利尔美术馆

Travelers in Snowy Mountains

Southern Song dynasty (1127–1279)
Artist unknown
Ink on silk
Album leaf
H×W : 24.3×25.7 cm
The Freer Gallery of Art
Gift of Charles Lang Freer

171. 夜潮图

南宋
佚名
绢本水墨
册页
纵22.2、横22.4厘米
大都会艺术博物馆

Waves in Moonlight

Southern Song dynasty (1127–1279)
Artist unknown
Ink on silk
Album leaf
H×W : 22.2×22.4 cm
The Metropolitan Museum of Art
From the Collection of A. W. Bahr,
Purchase, Fletcher Fund, 1947

172. 冬景图

南宋
佚名
绢本设色
册页
纵24.1、横24.8厘米
大都会艺术博物馆

Winter Landscape

Southern Song dynasty (1127–1279)
Artist unknown
Ink and color on silk
Album leaf
H×W : 24.1×24.8 cm
The Metropolitan Museum of Art
From the Collection of A. W. Bahr,
Purchase, Fletcher Fund, 1947

173. 观瀑图

南宋
佚名
绢本设色
册页
纵25.1、横25.7厘米
大都会艺术博物馆

Watching Waterfall

Southern Song dynasty (1127–1279)
Artist unknown
Ink and color on silk
Album leaf
H×W : 25.1×25.7 cm
The Metropolitan Museum of Art
Bequest of John M. Crawford Jr., 1988

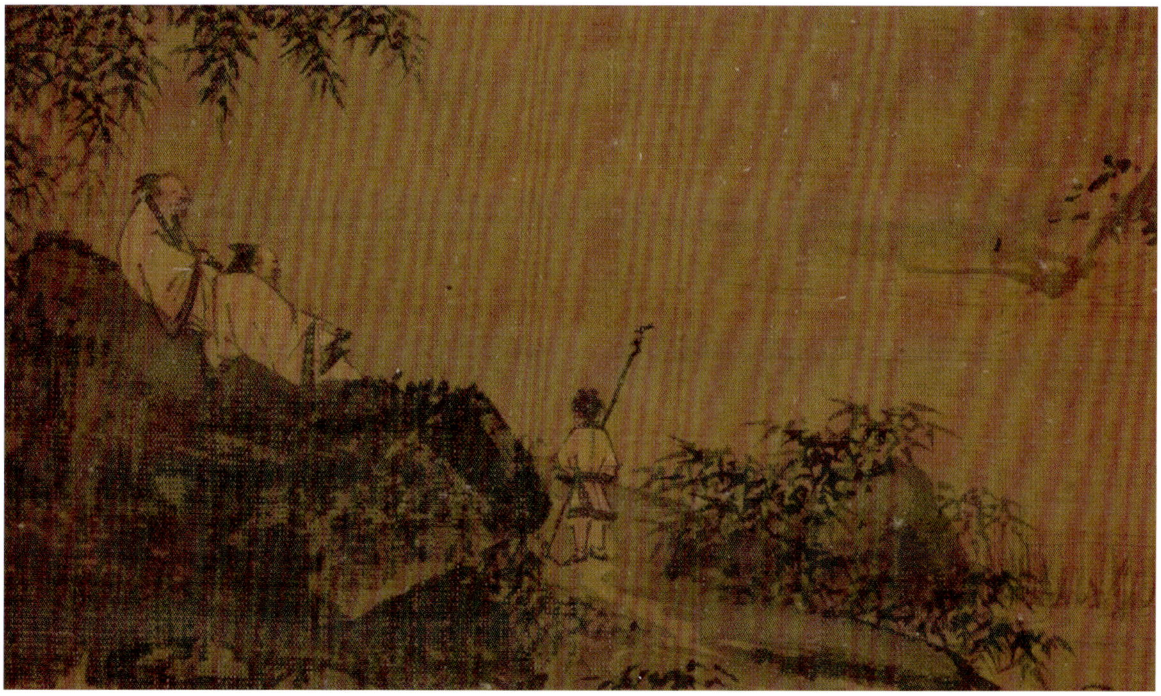

174. 柳荫策杖图

南宋
佚名
绢本设色
册页
纵23.6、横25.4厘米
哈佛艺术博物馆

Sage and Attendant Beneath Willow

Southern Song dynasty (1127–1279)
Artist unknown
Ink and color on silk
Album leaf
H×W : 23.6×25.4 cm
The Harvard Art Museums
Harvard Art Museums/Arthur M. Sackler Museum, Gift of Dr. Denman W. Ross
© President and Fellows of Harvard College

175. 湖畔庭院图

南宋
佚名
绢本设色
册页
纵26.9、横28.1厘米
弗利尔美术馆

Strolling to Lakeside Gazebo

Southern Song dynasty (1127–1279)
Artist unknown
Ink and color on silk
Album leaf
H×W : 26.9×28.1 cm
The Freer Gallery of Art
Gift of Charles Lang Freer

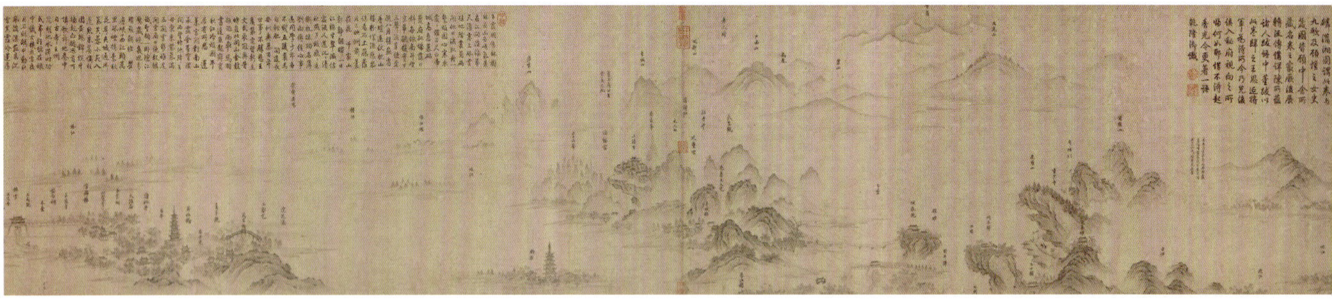

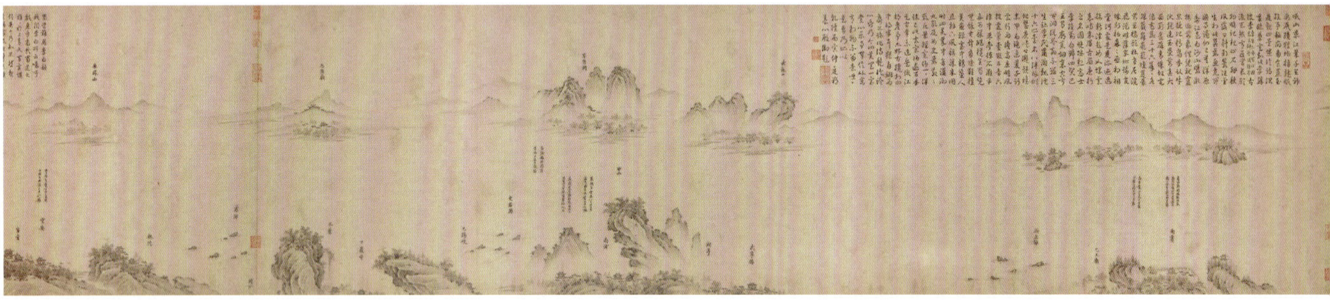

176. 蜀江图

南宋
佚名
纸本水墨
手卷
纵32.3、横752.1厘米
弗利尔美术馆

Shu River

Southern Song dynasty (1127–1279)
Artist unknown
Ink on paper
Handscroll
H×W : 32.3×752.1 cm
The Freer Gallery of Art
Gift of Charles Lang Freer

顧逵厨汝和客故藏有李龍眠瀟
湘蜀川二畫俱稱神品瀟湘畵歸
予吳吾嘗於吳氏見之同卿之名
恨不能已蜀川圖不忍釋手誰能
展玩相賞之蹄同卿今年秋
王海上予以七十壽公之夫者物
稿人事天地間原目瞬息況多秋
又生物而悲孚生一浮一澫之為用

此卷金潤之海上顧氏之藏
入吳迅捷軍秊湯湯楊央奉吉
臃□□李祝書 其昌

137

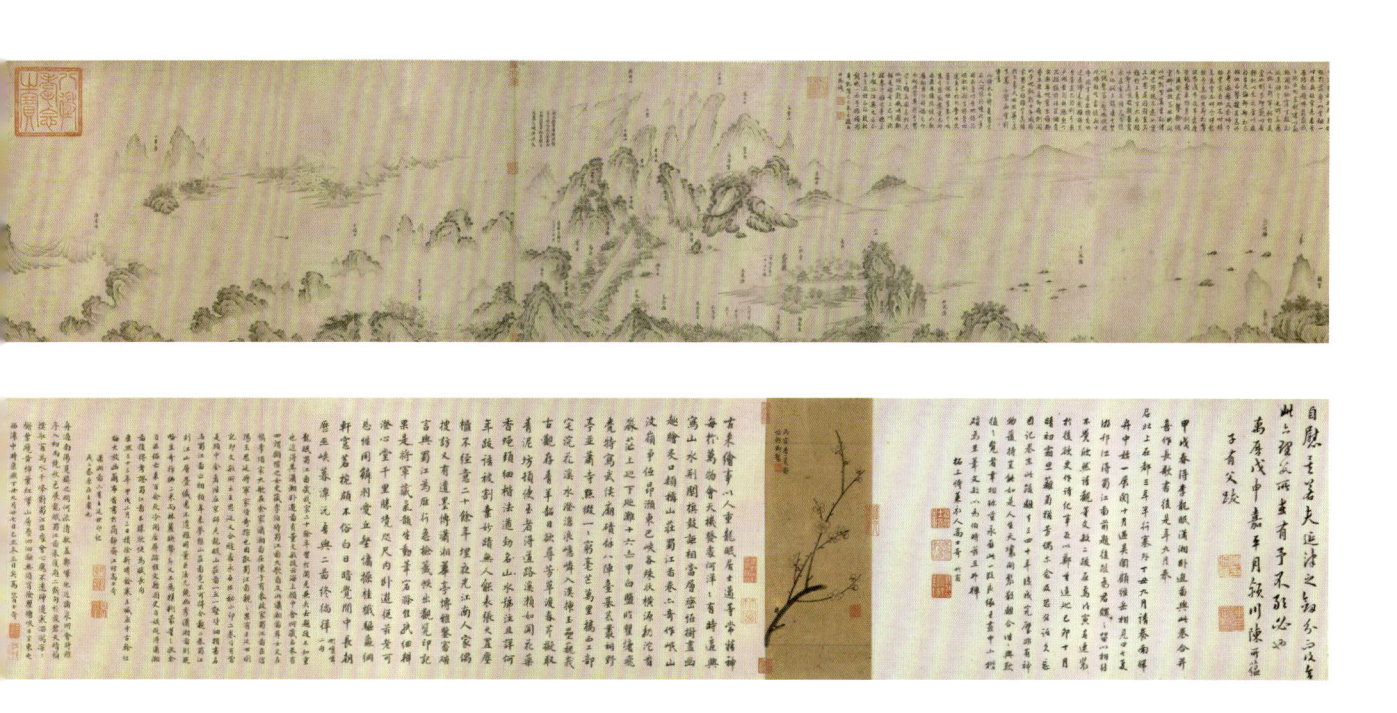

177. 观瀑图

南宋
佚名
绢本设色
册页
纵29.1、横27.6厘米
大都会艺术博物馆

Watching Waterfall

Southern Song dynasty (1127–1279)
Artist unknown
Ink and color on silk
Album leaf
H×W : 29.1×27.6 cm
The Metropolitan Museum of Art
Bequest of John M. Crawford Jr., 1988

178. 风雨归舟图

南宋
佚名
绢本设色
册页
纵24.8、横27.3厘米
大都会艺术博物馆

Returning Boat in Wind and Rain

Southern Song dynasty (1127–1279)
Artist unknown
Ink and color on silk
Album leaf
H×W : 24.8×27.3 cm
The Metropolitan Museum of Art
Bequest of John M. Crawford Jr., 1988

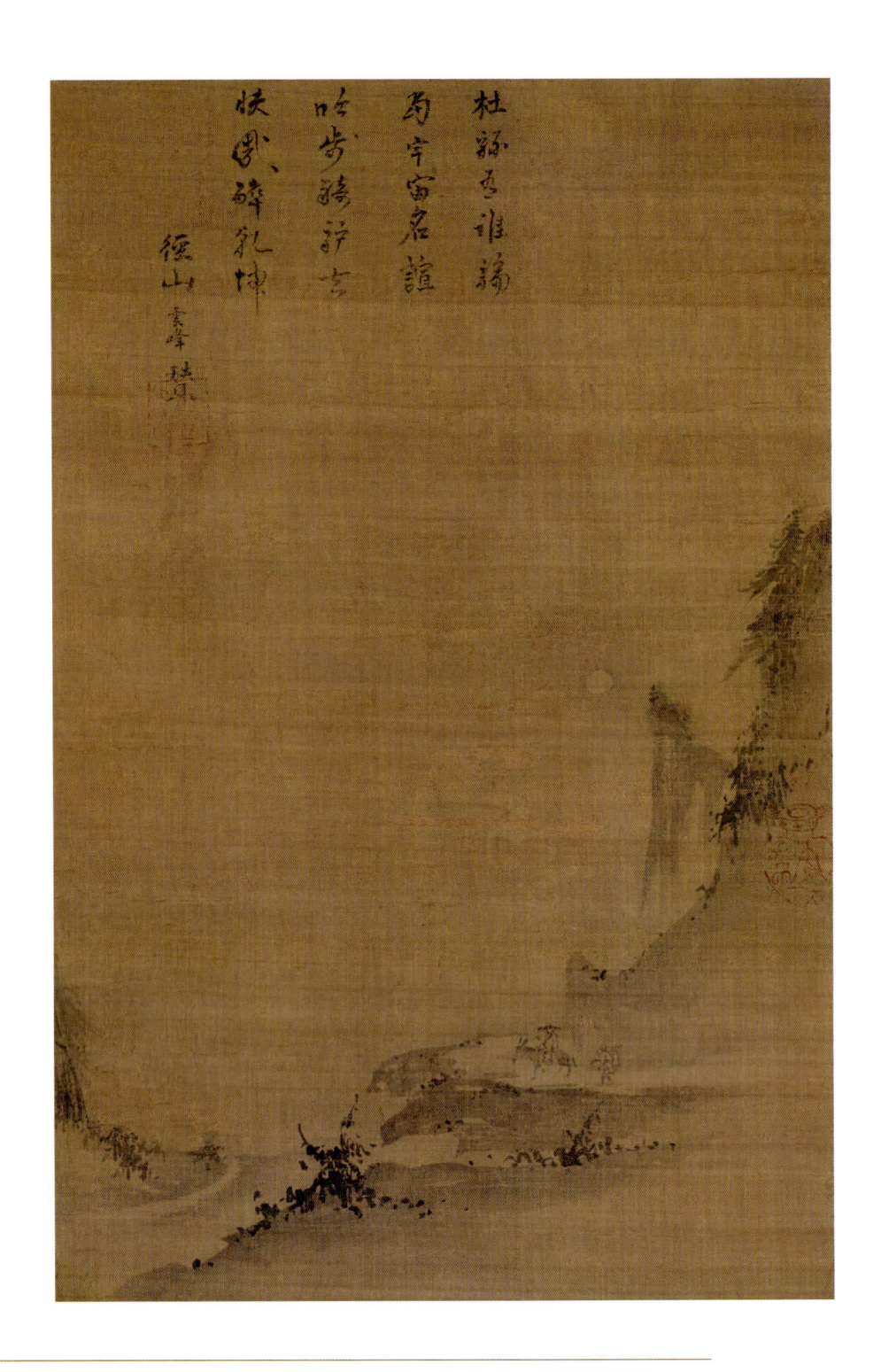

179. 山水图

Landscape

宋或元
佚名
绢本水墨
立轴
纵54.3、横36厘米
克利夫兰美术馆

Song dynasty (960–1279) or Yuan dynasty (1271–1368)
Artist unknown
Ink on silk
Hanging scroll
H×W : 54.3×36 cm
The Cleveland Museum of Art
Mr. and Mrs. William H. Marlatt Fund 1987.37

180. 幽禽寒林图

南宋
佚名
绢本设色
册页
纵23.8、横24.1厘米
大都会艺术博物馆

Two Birds on Wintry Tree

Southern Song dynasty (1127–1279)
Artist unknown
Ink and color on silk
Album leaf
H×W : 23.8×24.1 cm
The Metropolitan Museum of Art
Bequest of John M. Crawford Jr., 1988

181. 雪江待渡图

南宋
佚名
绢本水墨
册页
纵25.1、横25.7厘米
大都会艺术博物馆

Waiting for Ferry

Southern Song dynasty (1127–1279)
Artist unknown
Ink on silk
Album leaf
H×W : 25.1×25.7 cm
The Metropolitan Museum of Art
John Stewart Kennedy Fund, 1913

182. 冒雨寻庄图

南宋
佚名
绢本设色
册页
纵25.6、横26.4厘米
大都会艺术博物馆

Returning Home in Driving Rain

Southern Song dynasty (1127–1279)
Artist unknown
Ink and color on silk
Album leaf
H×W : 25.6×26.4 cm
The Metropolitan Museum of Art
Purchase, The Dillon Fund Gift, 1982

183. 春山图

南宋
佚名
绢本设色
册页
纵24.8、横26厘米
大都会艺术博物馆

Early Spring Landscape

Southern Song dynasty (1127–1279)
Artist unknown
Ink and color on silk
Album leaf
H×W : 24.8×26 cm
The Metropolitan Museum of Art
Bequest of John M. Crawford Jr., 1988

184. 江行图

宋或元
佚名
绢本水墨
册页
纵36、横40.9厘米
荷兰国立博物馆

Voyage Along the River

Song dynasty (960–1279) or Yuan dynasty (1271–1368)
Artist unknown
Ink on silk
Album leaf
H×W : 36×40.9 cm
The Rijksmuseum
On loan from the Royal Asian Art Society in The Netherlands (purchase Yokoyama, Kyoto, 1931)

185. 古柏归禽图

南宋
佚名
绢本水墨
册页
纵23.8、横24.9厘米
克利夫兰美术馆

Returning Birds and Old Cypress

Southern Song dynasty (1127–1279)
Artist unknown
Ink on silk
Album leaf
H×W : 23.8×24.9 cm
The Cleveland Museum of Art
Gift of Dr. and Mrs. Sherman E. Lee 1969.305

186. 花鸟图

南宋
佚名
绢本设色
册页
纵20、横22.5厘米
大都会艺术博物馆

Flower and Bird

Southern Song dynasty (1127–1279)
Artist unknown
Ink and color on silk
Album leaf
H×W : 20×22.5 cm
The Metropolitan Museum of Art
John Stewart Kennedy Fund, 1913

187. 梅花幽鸟图

南宋
佚名
绢本设色
册页
纵23.8、横24.5厘米
克利夫兰美术馆

Bird on Flowering Branch

Southern Song dynasty (1127–1279)
Artist unknown
Ink and color on silk
Album leaf
H×W : 23.8×24.5 cm
The Cleveland Museum of Art
The Kelvin Smith Collection, given by Mrs. Kelvin Smith 1985.371

188. 桃枝双鸟图

南宋
佚名
绢本设色
册页
纵24.8、横25.7厘米
克利夫兰美术馆

Birds on Peach Branch

Southern Song dynasty (1127–1279)
Artist unknown
Ink and color on silk
Album leaf
H×W : 24.8×25.7 cm
The Cleveland Museum of Art
The Kelvin Smith Collection, given by Mrs. Kelvin Smith 1985.367

189. 梅竹雀鸟图

南宋
佚名
绢本设色
册页
纵25.7、横26.7厘米
大都会艺术博物馆

Sparrows Plum Blossoms and Bamboo

Southern Song dynasty (1127–1279)
Artist unknown
Ink and color on silk
Album leaf
H×W : 25.7×26.7 cm
The Metropolitan Museum of Art
Bequest of Mary Clark Thompson, 1923

190. 三猿得鹭图

南宋
佚名
绢本设色
册页
纵24.1、横22.9厘米
大都会艺术博物馆

Gibbons Raiding Egret's Nest

Southern Song dynasty (1127–1279)
Artist unknown
Ink and color on silk
Album leaf
H×W : 24.1×22.9 cm
The Metropolitan Museum of Art
John Stewart Kennedy Fund, 1913

191. 芦塘鸥鹭图

南宋
佚名
绢本设色
册页
纵25.2、横26.2厘米
大都会艺术博物馆

Egrets in Water Reeds

Southern Song dynasty (1127–1279)
Artist unknown
Ink and color on silk
Album leaf
H×W : 25.2×26.2 cm
The Metropolitan Museum of Art
From the Collection of A. W. Bahr,
Purchase, Fletcher Fund, 1947

192. 牧牛图

南宋
佚名
绢本设色
册页
纵24.8、横24.2厘米
弗利尔美术馆

Water Buffalo, Calf and Herdboy

Southern Song dynasty (1127–1279)
Artist unknown
Ink and color on silk
Album leaf
H×W : 24.8×24.2 cm
The Freer Gallery of Art
Gift of Charles Lang Freer

193. 观梅图

宋或元
佚名
绢本设色
立轴
纵94.6、横29.2厘米
大都会艺术博物馆

Scholar Admiring Plum Blossoms

Song dynasty (960–1279) or Yuan dynasty (1271–1368)
Artist unknown
Ink and color on silk
Hanging scroll
H×W : 94.6×29.2 cm
The Metropolitan Museum of Art
Purchase, The Dillon Fund Gift, 1988

194. 红芍药图

宋
佚名
绢本设色
册页
纵23.8、横19.1厘米
大都会艺术博物馆

Peony Flower and Leaves

Song dynasty (960–1279)
Artist unknown
Ink and color on silk
Album leaf
H×W : 23.8×19.1 cm
The Metropolitan Museum of Art
Rogers Fund, 1923

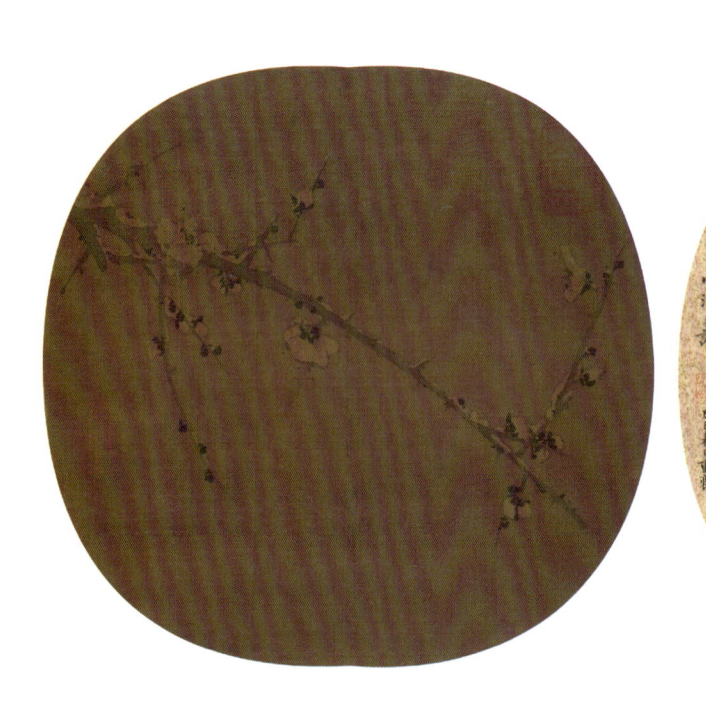

195. 腊梅图

宋
佚名
绢本水墨
册页
纵24.3、横25.4厘米
大都会艺术博物馆

Snow Plum

Song dynasty (960–1279)
Artist unknown
Ink on silk
Album leaf
H×W : 24.3×25.4 cm
The Metropolitan Museum of Art
From the Collection of A. W. Bahr,
Purchase, Fletcher Fund, 1947

196. 鼠食荔枝图

宋
佚名
绢本设色
册页
纵24.8、横25.2厘米
大都会艺术博物馆

Mouse Eating Lichee Fruit

Song dynasty (960–1279)
Artist unknown
Ink and color on silk
Album leaf
H×W : 24.8×25.2 cm
The Metropolitan Museum of Art
From the Collection of A. W. Bahr,
Purchase, Fletcher Fund, 1947

197. 秋瓜图

宋
佚名
绢本设色
册页
纵20.6、横23.8厘米
大都会艺术博物馆

Squash

Song dynasty (960–1279)
Artist unknown
Ink and color on silk
Album leaf
H×W : 20.6×23.8 cm
The Metropolitan Museum of Art
John Stewart Kennedy Fund, 1913

198. 雪雁图

南宋
佚名
绢本设色
册页
纵31.4、横28厘米
大都会艺术博物馆

Wild Geese in Winter

Southern Song dynasty (1127–1279)
Artist unknown
Ink and color on silk
Album leaf
H×W : 31.4×28 cm
The Metropolitan Museum of Art
From the Collection of A. W. Bahr,
Purchase, Fletcher Fund, 1947

199. 秋岸水鸟图

南宋
佚名
绢本设色
册页
纵22.4、横24厘米
克利夫兰美术馆

Birds on Autumn Inlet

Southern Song dynasty (1127–1279)
Artist unknown
Ink and color on silk
Album leaf
H×W : 22.4×24 cm
The Cleveland Museum of Art
The Kelvin Smith Collection, given by Mrs. Kelvin Smith 1985.369

200. 水仙图

宋或元
佚名
绢本设色
册页
纵23.8、横24.4厘米
大都会艺术博物馆

Narcissus

Song dynasty (960–1279) or Yuan dynasty (1271–1368)
Artist unknown
Ink and color on silk
Album leaf
H×W : 23.8×24.4 cm
The Metropolitan Museum of Art
John Stewart Kennedy Fund, 1913

201. 竹石图

宋或元
佚名
绢本水墨
立轴
纵47.5、横27厘米
克利夫兰美术馆

Bamboo Landscape

Song dynasty (960–1279) or Yuan dynasty (1271–1368)
Artist unknown
Ink on silk
Hanging scroll
H×W : 47.5×27 cm
The Cleveland Museum of Art
Mr. and Mrs. William H. Marlatt Fund

202. 雪岸寒鸦图

南宋
佚名
绢本设色
册页
纵26、横24.6厘米
克利夫兰美术馆

Birds and Ducks on Snowy Islet

Southern Song dynasty (1127–1279)
Artist unknown
Ink and color on silk
Album leaf
H×W : 26×24.6 cm
The Cleveland Museum of Art
Gift of the Womens Council of The Cleveland Museum of Art 1961.260

203. 玉兰栖禽图

南宋
佚名
绢本设色
团扇
纵23.2、横24.8厘米
波士顿艺术博物馆

Bird on Flowering Branch

Southern Song dynasty (1127–1279)
Artist unknown
Ink and color on silk
Round fan
H×W : 23.2×24.8 cm
The Museum of Fine Arts, Boston
Chinese and Japanese Special Fund
© 2024 Museum of Fine Arts, Boston

204. 寒林归鸦图

南宋
佚名
绢本设色
团扇
纵23.2、横25厘米
波士顿艺术博物馆

Flock of Birds Returning to Wintry Woods

Southern Song dynasty (1127–1279)
Artist unknown
Ink and color on silk
Round fan
H×W : 23.2×25 cm
The Museum of Fine Arts, Boston
Chinese and Japanese Special Fund
© 2024 Museum of Fine Arts, Boston

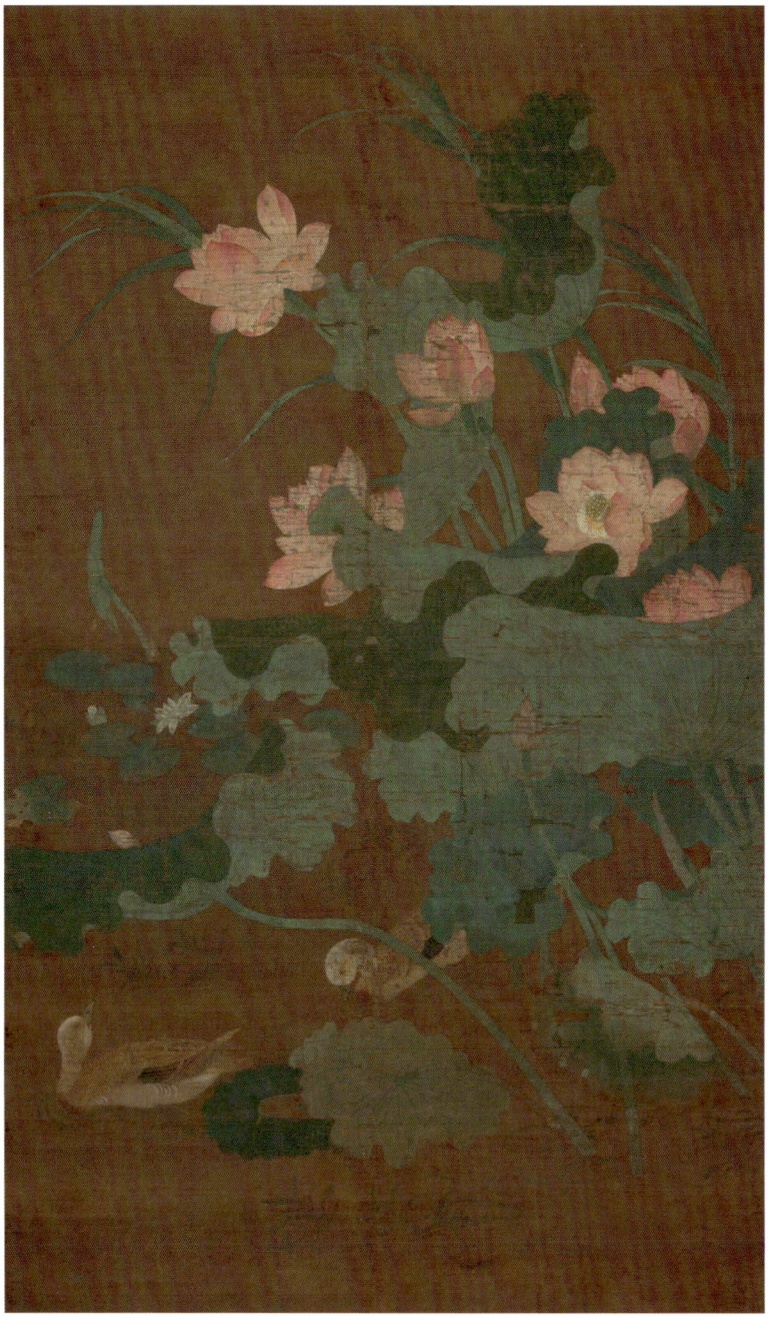

205. 莲池水禽图

宋或元
佚名
绢本设色
立轴
每联：纵150.3、横90.9厘米
东京国立博物馆

Lotus Pond and Waterfowl

Song dynasty (960–1279) or Yuan dynasty (1271–1368)
Artist unknown
Ink and color on silk
Handing scroll
H×W(each leaf) : 150.3×90.9 cm
The Tokyo National Museum
ColBase(https://colbase.nich.go.jp/collection_items/tnm/TA-142?locale=ja)

167

206. 墨竹图

宋或元
佚名
绢本水墨
立轴
纵91.2、横39.8厘米
克利夫兰美术馆

Ink Bamboo

Song dynasty (960–1279) or Yuan dynasty (1271–1368)
Artist unknown
Ink on silk
Hanging scroll
H×W : 91.2×39.8 cm
The Cleveland Museum of Art
John L. Severance Fund 1982.138

207. 枇杷八哥图

宋或元
佚名
绢本设色
册页
纵31.1、横31.1厘米
大都会艺术博物馆

Minah Bird on Loquat Branch

Song dynasty (960–1279) or Yuan dynasty (1271–1368)
Artist unknown
Ink and color on silk
Album leaf
H×W : 31.1×31.1 cm
The Metropolitan Museum of Art
John Stewart Kennedy Fund, 1913

208. 犬图

北宋
佚名
绢本设色
册页
纵22.6、横22.6厘米
克利夫兰美术馆

Dog Watching

Northern Song dynasty (960–1127)
Artist unknown
Ink and color on silk
Album leaf
H×W: 22.6×22.6 cm
The Cleveland Museum of Art
Gift of the John Huntington Art and
Polytechnic Trust 1915.700

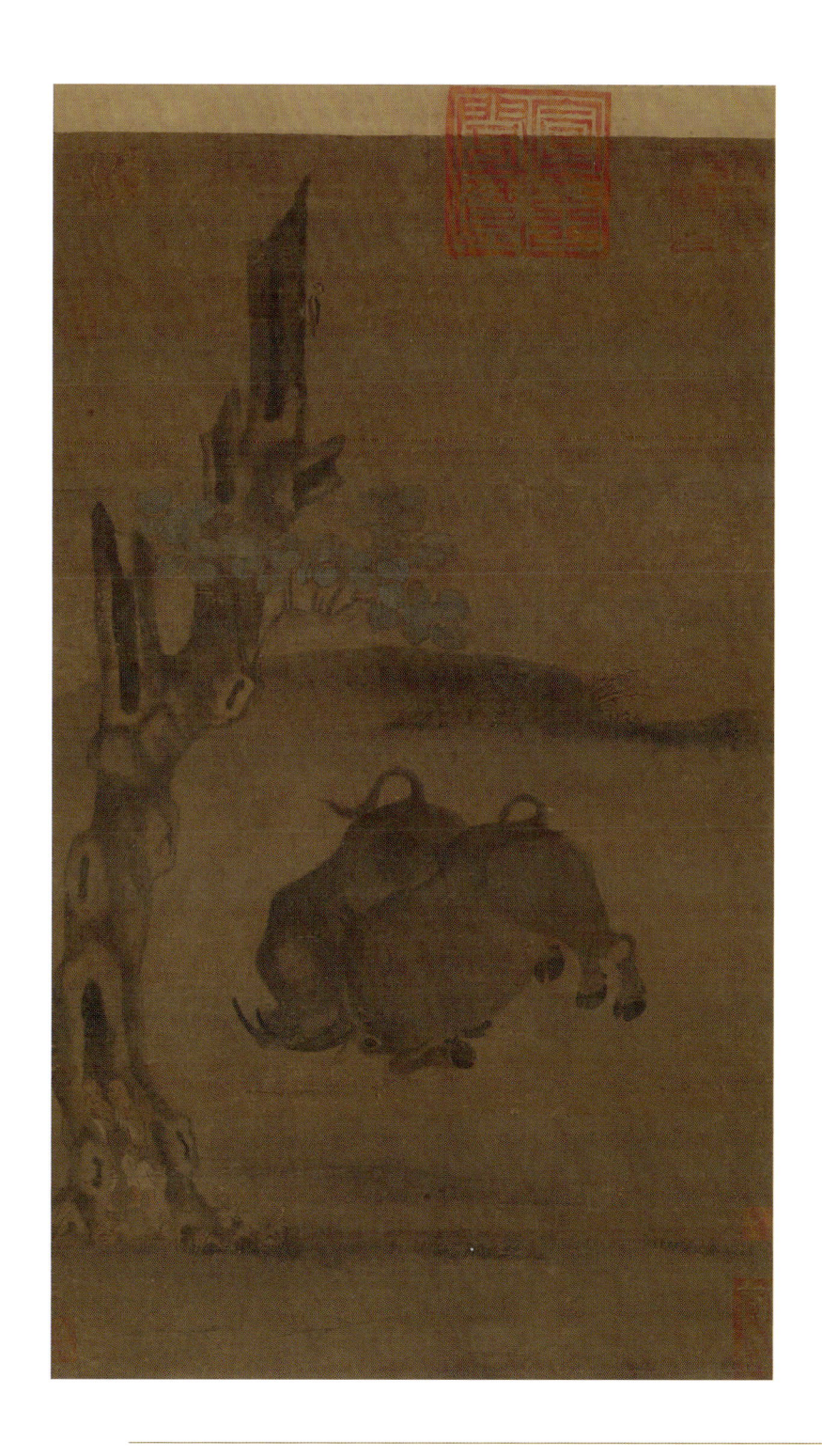

209. 斗牛图

宋或元
佚名
绢本设色
立轴
纵148、横74厘米
弗利尔美术馆

Two Fighting Water Buffaloes

Song dynasty (960–1279) or Yuan dynasty (1271–1368)
Artist unknown
Ink and color on silk
Hanging scroll
H×W : 148×74 cm
The Freer Gallery of Art
Gift of Ruth Meyer Epstein

210. 竹虫图

Insects and Bamboo

宋或元
佚名
绢本设色
册页
纵23.8、横25.6厘米
克利夫兰美术馆

Song dynasty (960–1279) or Yuan dynasty (1271–1368)
Artist unknown
Ink and color on silk
Album leaf
H×W : 23.8×25.6 cm
The Cleveland Museum of Art
The Kelvin Smith Collection, given by Mrs. Kelvin Smith 1985.364

211. 猿鹿图

南宋
佚名
绢本设色
册页
纵17.8、横22.2厘米
大都会艺术博物馆

Gibbons and Deer

Southern Song dynasty (1127–1279)
Artist unknown
Ink and color on silk
Album leaf
H×W : 17.8×22.2 cm
The Metropolitan Museum of Art
Edward Elliott Family Collection,
Purchase, The Dillon Fund Gift, 1982

朱家華山中日當煙靄雨笠
掛書牛角與童牧田野間或鳥
犍磧首或老特卧喧寄若起顧
而長鳴復表驅首而得杙狃影
此卷之人觀之有愍媿昔於此畫
家出獵茶其辟首犹掌之際
老作芳紛家以竜矮健東必然
㤀理與夫犵拒甬於亨岸者順
苜貼尾弰毅之三曲率其妙
笑蒡戴公藁世而勲自見翁
於巫於烏呼今四郊多難紀乃
港瀆肩虎不保筋苜之亦且尚
未已筅物之失宅僅秉又豈止乎
牛而巳笺又敢以奥予呓史
新安王逴題

212. 百牛图

宋或元
佚名
纸本水墨
手卷
纵31.8、横221.8厘米
大都会艺术博物馆

One Hundred Water Buffalo

Song dynasty (960–1279) or Yuan dynasty (1271–1368)
Artist unknown
Ink on paper
Handscroll
H×W : 31.8×221.8 cm
The Metropolitan Museum of Art
Rogers Fund, 1918

213. 仙驭奇禽图

南宋
佚名
绢本设色
册页
纵22.5、横22.5厘米
耶鲁大学艺术博物馆

Immortal Riding Dragon

Southern Song dynasty (1127–1279)
Artist unknown
Ink and color on silk
Album leaf
H×W : 22.5×22.5 cm
The Yale University Art Gallery
Gift of Dr. Howard Balensweig, B.S. 1943, and Mrs. Carolyn Balensweig

版权支持

（按中文馆名音序排列）

鲍尔基金会鲍氏东方艺术馆
贝纳基博物馆
波士顿艺术博物馆
不列颠博物馆
大阪市立东洋陶瓷美术馆
大阪市立美术馆
大都会艺术博物馆
东京国立博物馆
费城艺术博物馆
菲尔德博物馆
弗利尔美术馆
弗利尔与赛克勒美术馆
哈佛艺术博物馆
荷兰国立博物馆
集美博物馆
金贝尔艺术博物馆
凯布朗利博物馆
克利夫兰艺术博物馆
科隆东亚艺术博物馆
洛杉矶郡艺术博物馆
明尼阿波利斯美术馆
奈良国立博物馆
普林斯顿大学美术馆
赛克勒博物馆
赛克勒美术馆
圣路易斯艺术博物馆
维多利亚和阿尔伯特博物馆
新南威尔士州美术馆
辛辛那提艺术博物馆
亚洲文明博物馆
耶鲁大学艺术博物馆
印第安纳波利斯艺术博物馆
芝加哥艺术博物馆

Image Contributors

(In Chinese Pinyin Order)

The Baur Foundation, Museum of Far Eastern Art
The Benaki Museum
The Museum of Fine Arts, Boston
The British Museum
The Museum of Oriental Ceramics, Osaka
The Osaka City Museum of Fine Arts
The Metropolitan Museum of Art
The Tokyo National Museum
The Philadelphia Museum of Art
The Field Museum
The Freer Gallery of Art
The Freer and the Arthur M. Sackler Gallery
The Harvard Art Museums
The Rijksmuseum
The Guimet Museum
The Kimbell Art Museum
The Quai Branly Museum
The Cleveland Museum of Art
The Museum of East Asian Art, Cologne
The Los Angeles County Museum of Art
The Minneapolis Institute of Art
The Nara National Museum
The Princeton University Art Museum
The Arthur M. Sackler Museum
The Arthur M. Sackler Gallery
The Saint Louis Art Museum
The Victoria and Albert Museum
The Art Gallery of New South Wales
The Cincinnati Art Museum
The Asian Civilisations Museum
The Yale University Art Gallery
The Indianapolis Museum of Art
The Art Institute of Chicago

编辑、出版人员

总 策 划　马汝军　谢　刚
选题策划　孙志鹏
主任编辑　邹懿男
出版统筹　丁　宁

责任编辑　李文彧　林　琳
特约编辑　丁文文
编　　辑　陈　雯　张小君　汪　欣　孙立英　白华召　施　然　马　源
　　　　　赵笑笑　刘　琦　黄　艳　王　萌　王颖洁　王宏亮　毕力格图
责任校对　刘　义
实习编辑　齐倩颖　潘泓瑾

英文翻译　丁文文　耿玮浩
英文审校　韩　华

装帧设计　冷暖儿
图文版式　魏　丹　杨　丹　阮鸽鸽
责任印制　韦　舰　李珊珊

Editorial Staff

Chief Publisher   Ma Rujun   Xie Gang

Publisher   Sun Zhipeng

Editorial Director   Zou Yinan

Publishing Coordinator   Ding Ning

Editors-in-Charge   Li Wenyu   Lin Lin

Contributing Editor   Ding Wenwen

Editors   Chen Wen   Zhang Xiaojun   Wang Xin   Sun Liying   Bai Huazhao   Shi Ran   Ma Yuan   Zhao Xiaoxiao   Liu Qi   Huang Yan   Wang Meng   Wang Yingjie   Wang Hongliang   Biligt

Responsible Proofreader   Liu Yi

Interns   Qi Qianying   Pan Hongjin

English Translators   Ding Wenwen   Geng Weihao

English Proofreader   Han Hua

Cover Designer   Leng Nuaner

Layout Designers   Wei Dan   Yang Dan   Ruan Gege

Responsible Printing Coordinators   Wei Jian   Li Shanshan